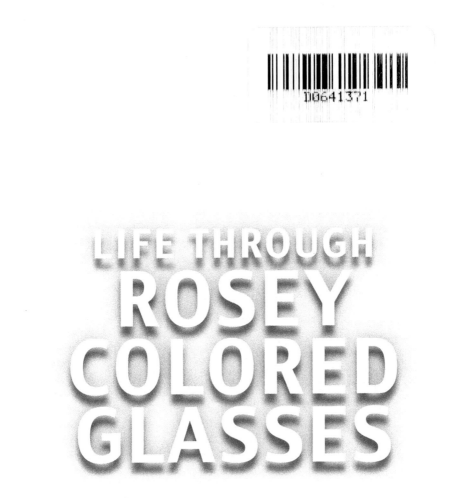

LIFE THROUGH ROSEY COLORED GLASSES

ROSEY GRIER

Trilogy Christian Publishers A Wholly Owned Subsidary of Trinity Broadcasting Network2442 Michelle Drive Tustin, CA 92780

Copyright © 2018 by Rosey Grier

All Scripture quotations, unless otherwise noted, taken from *THE HOLY BIBLE, NEW INTERNATIONAL VERSION®*, NIV® Copyright © 1973, 1978, 1984, 2011 by Biblica, Inc.® Used by permission. All rights reserved worldwide.

Scripture quotations marked (KJV) taken from *The Holy Bible, King James Version*. Cambridge Edition: 1769.

All rights reserved, including the right to reproduce this book or portions thereof in any form whatsoever. For information, address Trilogy Christian Publishing Rights Department, 2442 Michelle Drive, Tustin, Ca 92780.

First Trilogy Christian Publishing hardcover edition May 2018

Trilogy Christian Publishing/ TBN and colophon are trademarks of Trinity Broadcasting Network.

For information about special discounts for bulk purchases, please contact Trilogy Christian Publishing.

Manufactured in the United States of America

10 9 8 7 6 5 4 3 2 1

Library of Congress Cataloging-in-Publication Data is available.

ISBN 9781640880030 ISBN 9781640880382 (ebook)

Dedication

First of all, I would like to thank God for giving me the opportunity to experience all the things that made this book possible.

I want to dedicate this book to all the wonderful people who have been a part of my life down every road I walked, every field I played on, and every conversation that I've had. They all impressed me and had a meaningful impact on my life. If I tried to name all the people, I would have pages of individuals.

To my son, Roosevelt K. Grier, Jr., for his never-ending support and encouragement. To my friends, relatives, and acquaintances, I know you understand how easy you are to love and to care about. We've all been on the road of life and we've experienced good and bad times, but we're still moving forward and we shall run the whole race together to the end...then we will know what life is all about.

To all my grandchildren, your love is so special. I pray that you will travel the road in safety in the full armor of God and let your life be significant to all you meet. To my brothers and sisters, especially Eva, the devil is always out there doing his job, but we all know that he loses in the end.

And especially, thank you to Lady Cydnee, my wife. You picked me up when I was deep in the wilderness, and you led me like a blind man back to the light.

Table of Contents

Foreword

Chaplain Susan Stafford, Ph.D.
Original hostess of *Wheel of Fortune*

Rosey, Rosey, Rosey...

Rosey is known as the Gentle Giant with a holy calm. Gentle because he knows that love can overcome hate. As a Giant, he stands head and shoulders above most of us, but stoops low enough to whisper encouragement to a child. To quote Mark Twain, "Kindness is a language the deaf can hear and the blind can see."

Born in Georgia as one of 11 children, imagine the name his parents chose—Roosevelt. Out of respect for the president of the United States, they named their son in honor of FDR (President Franklin Delano Roosevelt).

Rosey's accomplishments are many, and to whom much is given, much is expected. Whether on the line with football's famous Fearsome Foursome, acting, singing, speaking, writing a book or believe it or not, even needlepoint, Rosey gives his all. I admire his big heart, which reaches out to so many as I've watched him work in the trenches and never complain. It doesn't matter if he's working with the Kennedys or the Smiths, people respect Rosey because of the caliber of his character. He started out by helping in his own community and continues to make a difference on a global scale.

Since the Master came into his life, Rosey's total focus has been on Jesus Christ, and his heart is that of a servant. Rosey always reminds us, "United we stand, divided we fall." Our nation needs this now more than ever.

Georgia has given us other great men, especially that of the remarkable Martin Luther King, Jr. This Gentle Giant heartily agrees with one of Dr. King's many quotes: "The ultimate measure of a man is not where he stands in moments of comfort and convenience, but where he stands at times of challenge and controversy."

Rosey Grier has lived his life helping to dispel the darkness and is my sacred friend as well as my brother. Helen Keller said, "It's really sad when people who can see have no vision." That certainly doesn't apply to my friend. Rosey helped to open my eyes and improve my sight for which I am most grateful. Rosey's goal is to finish this race with His grace. When the world is the darkest is when you need Agape love the most. And as iron sharpens iron, I pray your heart will be touched as mine has with Rosey's incredible journey.

Introduction

Roosevelt "Rosey" Grier

"There are those who look at things the way they are, and ask why... I dream of things that never were, and ask why not?"

—Robert Kennedy

Even though my sport was football, it seems to me that life is more like a baseball game. Sometimes it basically seems to "throw itself" at us. It throws us fastballs. Curve balls. Sliders. Pitches that are so far outside the strike zone there is no way anyone could possibly hit them. Pitches that are right over the plate and have "home run" written all over them. Yet, we can still miss those.

Our job, then, is to be as prepared for what comes our way as we possibly can be.

When we strike out, we can get another "at bat" in another inning. We can learn from our mistakes and move forward. When we get thrown out in a double play, we can come back with a grand slam home run a couple of innings later.

I call this simple illustration "seeing life through Rosey-colored glasses." Others know it by other terms—faith and hope. And even "optimism" or "seeing the glass as half full."

My primary purpose in writing this book is to demonstrate that no matter what life pitches to you, you can still take a swing, get a hit, and score a run—or two or three, or even get that grand slam.

Yes, life comes at all of us with surprises…with uncertainties that can derail us. In the pages that follow, you will see that I have experienced my share of setbacks. Disappointments. Even deep hurts.

Sometimes, I think that I just may have "seen it all."

I was born in the deep South. I've labored in hot cotton fields, and I've shaken peanuts under the blazing sun. Yet, I've seen the beauty of hope in my parents—who wanted more for their children than what we were born into. That helped me look at life through Rosey-colored glasses.

I've seen the ugly face of racial hatred. But I've also seen the faces of people of all races who reject racism in favor of love. Another reason to see life through those Rosey-colored lenses.

I've seen the promise of a brighter future in the mind and heart of Robert F. Kennedy. Then, I saw that promise destroyed by an assassin's hatred as I stood by and watched helplessly. But still, I hoped. I put on my glasses…

I was right there years ago when my young son, Lil' Ro, Jr., said something like, "Dad, can we go to church?" I said, "No." I hadn't been to church in 20 years. His reply was, "But I've never been to church." That gripped my heart.

I've followed several men into prison and tried my best to give hope. There are many people who would argue that they deserved nothing.

Just like my life in the NFL, I've seen wins, losses, injuries, and healing in "real life." Thankfully, along the way, I've had some important lessons on how to play the game.

When I played football in high school, in college, and in the pros, I had coaches. These were experienced men who knew the rules of the game, knew how to design plays—both on offense and defense—and knew how to build teams. At the same time, they knew how to bring out the best in each player.

I've never been a coach myself. But I've watched the great ones…while I was playing and since then. I've studied them. They seem to have several things in common. They are inspiring, they are demanding, they are supportive, and they are both forgiving and unforgiving. They are tolerant of sincere mistakes, and intolerant of stupid ones.

And that's exactly what life is. Life, in the form of the people you meet, can be inspiring, demanding, supportive, forgiving and unforgiving. People can be tolerant at times, intolerant at other times.

Life comes at us full force, much like an offensive line or wide receivers looking for an open space for a big catch. That can be very intimidating, but it's our job to get off the bench and head out onto the field to play the game—and stop the drive.

With competent coaching—and your very best efforts...and those of your teammates—you can prevent the score and get the ball back.

That's one of the most important things I've learned my 80-plus years of life. That and other significant "self-discoveries" form the basis of this book. But this is not an autobiography in the strictest sense of the word. Although I will naturally relate some of the more significant events in my life, my story is more about what my dear friend, Bobby Kennedy, described as the "why's" and the "why not's," and less about the "Who's, What's, When's and Where's."

Ultimately, it is my hope that you, too, will discover that all of life is more exciting and promising when you look at it through Rosey-colored glasses!

Rosey's Rose-Colored Gem

I'm going to end each chapter with a brief, straightforward "lesson" that I hope you will be able to apply to your day. The first one is very simple: "You can't win in life if you don't suit up. So get out there and play!"

Chapter One

Born for a Reason

"Men are born to succeed, not to fail."

—Henry David Thoreau

A Southern-born, 5-year-old Black boy could learn a lot about life while he's picking cotton under the boiling sun.

He could learn to be resentful. To disrespect—if not hate—the White people who somehow still think they own him, decades after slavery was abolished.

Or he could have hope. He could have faith that somehow things could and will be better for him someday.

He could lay back, be a slacker, and not care about much of anything. Or he could be a 5-year-old kid who keeps up with the adults working the field with him…and even outperforms some of them. He could actually get paid full adult wages because his hard work was noticed and appreciated.

He could become a cynic. He could get angry about every injustice he sees…and carry that anger around with him. Or he could learn about the Love of God and the good that other people do to heal the world, because their hearts are in the right place and they clearly display both hope and faith.

I believe I was born to have hope and faith. I believe I was born to serve others. At one time, I believed that I could and should take the pain of others on myself, and that sent me into a depression.

This all happened in an America that didn't especially welcome me with open arms. Or expect me to get an education. Or believe that I could be a success. This all happened in an America that expected me to pick cotton and sing Negro Spirituals. "Nobody knows the trouble I've seen…nobody knows but Jesus."

When you finish reading my words, some of you might think that I have every right to disrespect America…to hate where I came from and what I've witnessed in my life. After all, I saw my share of poverty. I was the object of scorn and ridicule and racism when I played college football…until I proved myself through determination and hard work. And I watched in absolute horror and disbelief as a young Senator who could have been a promising president was gunned down within a few feet of me.

Some of my African-American readers may criticize me because they think I may have sold out to White America. That I played their game and didn't do enough for "my" people.

Here's what I want you to know. My story is about an American who loves America and cares about all of us, no matter what color or faith or level of education or economic status.

My story is about victories and defeats, highs and lows, successes and failures, accomplishments and regrets, wins and losses, and the good and the not so good. If it seems to you as though I just said the same thing six ways, you're right! That's what life is all about for most of us, isn't it?

Even the 1972 Miami Dolphins, who had the NFL's only undefeated season and won the Super Bowl, had experienced defeats before that season…and many more since. They were only "perfect" for one season. (I promise you that this won't turn into a football book, although I just *might* mention my NFL years a couple times. After all, this *is* my story.)

My story is not going to be filled with anger or bitterness. I have always lived my life to create the new, rather than destroy the old—to build bridges rather than burning them.

I try to live a positive life, even if it means that I sometimes have to minimize the negative. We all get to choose our attitude, and, hopefully, the truth will stand and eliminate the lies. That's why I prefer to look at life through my Rosey-colored glasses.

One of the biggest lessons I learned as a young boy was that I had a role to play. I was "number nine" among the thirteen children to whom my mother had given birth. Not all survived, but as kids in a family that was struggling for survival, we were all considered to be part of the "team." So, my role, then, was to help us survive.

I didn't know at the time that my role was so large. So important. So essential. I just knew that I had a personal goal. And that was to prove myself. It was an important "life lesson" that I was just beginning to discover, but learning and applying that lesson has served me well.

Even though my dad wasn't an educated man in the traditional sense, he was one of the wisest people I have ever known. His wisdom wasn't revealed through brilliant writing or spellbinding oratory. It was dispensed through short, concise "gems," in some ways very similar to the gems I share at the end of each chapter.

Here's one of Dad's—and it took the form of a warning. He said, "Trouble is easy to get into and hard to get out of. The best thing to do is stay out of trouble."

On the surface, this sounds like simple, homespun advice. But think about how this thought could apply in our world today: "A war is easy to get into and hard to get out of. The best thing to do is to not go to war." Consider Vietnam, Iraq, and Afghanistan for a moment, and this point becomes vividly clear.

Growing up in Georgia, I had plenty of opportunity to heed my dad's advice.

My two favorite weekly "events" were going to town on Friday or Saturday nights (a 10-mile ride on a rough-riding horse-drawn wagon that took us close to two hours), or staying home while my parents went to town. When we kids stayed home, my older brothers and I would find creative ways to get in trouble. It wasn't huge trouble, but it was trouble nonetheless.

Of course, of all the options we had for trouble, our dad's 12-gauge shotgun was at the top of the list. I was a big kid at 5 years of age, so I convinced my brothers that I could handle the big shotgun. I couldn't. The recoil knocked me to the ground. I was humiliated. Luckily, my brothers somehow understood my situation, and they taught me how to hold the gun so as not to get knocked down every time I pulled the trigger.

We would usually shoot into the air—not a safe practice by any means—but one time I was shooting with a friend and we fired in the direction of a sound and shot a pig. We didn't mean to kill it on purpose, but I still got a whipping with a rope. My cohort in crime, John Arthur Wilson, is still my friend to this day. (In fact, he moved to New Jersey at the same time my family did. More on that later.)

Nights at home when our parents weren't there wasn't always fun for me, especially if my older brother, Arthur, was around. He had a temper. He used to beat me up and bang my head on the ground—and I really don't think I deserved that!

We had a tin roof on our barn, and the older kids would slide off the roof and land in a pile of hay on the ground. Arthur decided it would be amusing to make a little kid—me—do the same thing the older ones did. So he forced me to slide off the roof, and I had a hard landing.

"I'm gonna tell papa what you made me do," I threatened.

"No, you're not," he shot back. And, of course, he'd jump on me.

I had a good kick for a young guy, so I kicked him as hard as I could and took off. I ran into the house and explained to my sisters what had just happened. My sister Eula would take Arthur's side, and Eva would take my side.

Then I'd wait for Arthur to come inside, and I'd kick him again.

As much fun as tangling with my brother and shooting the shotgun were, the real treat for this farm boy was going to town. My parents would give each of us a nickel—or a quarter if they were feeling especially generous. That quarter could get us into a movie and buy a soda, or I could spend it on crackers or white bread and sardines…my favorites. It had to be white bread, because mom made wheat bread at home. That made white bread special!

I would buy a loaf of bread and a can of sardines, sit down in the park in the center of our small town, and eat the whole thing. Yes, people laughed at me! But I didn't mind—I was having the treat of my life!

The fun thing about going to town is that, for the next week, I had something to talk about with my friends.

There was one time, though, that I didn't want to talk about what happened in town. We had gone to town, and of course, I bought my sardines and white bread, and I was enjoying my "snack." Out of nowhere, a man started yelling at Arthur. Now, Arthur was a big, strong, fast guy, (with a temper, as I mentioned) so it was not a good idea to mess with him. Arthur got mad and decided to chase after the guy.

In the midst of all this commotion, someone near us took out a big shotgun, loaded the chamber with a shell, and shot and killed a man. He was gunned down right in front of us. The crowd, of course, scattered as fast as possible.

I looked at the man on the ground. His leg was twitching and he was bleeding profusely, yet no one was rushing over to do anything to help him. It was the first time I watched a man die at the hands of a gunman. But it wouldn't be the last.

My brother was unbelievably angry when we headed back home that night. He wasn't upset with the man who had shot someone on the street. He was furious with the guy who had "embarrassed" him, so he decided he was going to "get him."

We snuck in the house as quietly as we could. Arthur grabbed my dad's shotgun. We went to the guy's house and sat in the dark a few yards away from his front door, waiting for him to come outside at night. We were there all night long waiting…waiting… waiting.

The reason I went with Arthur was because I wasn't going to let him do anything bad. He thought I was going to help him out, but I was there to try to stop him.

Naturally, I couldn't stop him if I wasn't with him, and I knew if I told him what I was going to do, he wouldn't have let me come with him.

The guy never came outside, so we eventually went home. That was a good thing, because I wasn't ready to watch another man die that night.

But I learned something through this experience…sitting in the dark with my brother. I learned that saving lives just might be something we all can do…whether it's feeding a homeless person or being a "Good Samaritan" at the scene of an accident.

Or whether it's giving blood to the Red Cross or making sure that "Organ Donor" is checked on our driver's licenses.

That night, in my young mind, a significant thought was just beginning to take form: *There might be a reason...a purpose...behind my life.*

Rosey's Rose-Colored Gem

We all have a purpose—and an ultimate destiny. I believe that our purpose is inspired by those who influence our lives. Our parents. Our families. Our teachers. Our peers.
But our destiny is a gift of God's intention. Our destiny is our ultimate destination.

Chapter Two

Book Learning

"Being ignorant is not so much a shame, as being unwilling to learn."

—Benjamin Franklin

Until I was eight-years-old, Cuthbert, Georgia, was all I knew about life. About the world. About people. I didn't know there would—or could—be anything more.

Cuthbert is a small city in—and the county seat of—Randolph County, in the southwest corner of Georgia. The population in 2010 was 3,873 but in 1932, when I was born, it was much smaller.

I grew up in a predominantly Black area. I had a few White friends, but Cuthbert was completely segregated back then. My family went to a Black church, and I attended an all-Black school.

I was baptized when I was only 7 years old. I had no idea what "baptized" meant, what being a "Baptist" meant, or why all of this was important. All I knew is that I was dunked in a nearby creek, and I thought that made me a Baptist. I wasn't able, at my young age, to make any sort of connection with "Christian." It would take me decades to know what that word meant.

Growing up as a young child in Georgia, I must have been viewed by my friends as an "oddball." For the most part, they hated school and loved summer vacation. I was the opposite. While I enjoyed summer vacation, I preferred to be in school. I loved learning.

Sadly, I didn't have as much of an opportunity to learn as I wanted. There was always work to be done on the farm, and we weren't among those well-off farm families who could afford a hired hand. Why would my dad even consider that? After all, of the eleven kids my parents had, there were seven of us living at home.

In most families in the South in the 1930s—whether they were Black or White—education held very little importance. Sweating in the fields…helping your family grow food and make an income…was the priority.

What that meant to me was that I could only attend school three days a week. I fell seriously behind my peers as a result.

By most standards, I wasn't a good student. I wasn't even average. But I excelled in one area. I had desire. I wanted to learn. You heard of "E" for Effort? I was Effort with a huge capital E.

Many of my lessons in life, though, came from my world outside of school. My dad—I called him "Poppa"—was a man of courage and character. Living in the South could be intimidating. It wasn't that many years after the Civil War, and many White folks didn't see us as emancipated. As free. They thought Abraham Lincoln has made a huge mistake, and that the South would always be the South they knew.

Their views didn't intimidate my Poppa, though. While many Blacks wouldn't look Whites in the eye, my dad didn't have that issue. He would look anyone, Black or White, in the eye and speak his mind. I learned much about my value as a human being from that giant of a man!

As my older siblings grew older, they left the farm, one by one. Arthur and I were the only boys who were still home. That didn't last long, because when Arthur turned 13, he married a beautiful girl named Bertha May. Even at my young age, I was jealous, because she was exactly the kind of girl I thought I would one day marry myself. In fact, secretly, I hoped she would wait for me. I've always had big dreams!

My dad was worried that I'd be the next to run off and get married, but at 8 years of age, there was little chance of that!

I would try to reassure him: "No, Poppa, I will always be here for you."

With Arthur and the other boys gone, I had to take on more responsibility. It was a lot for a young boy, and it also cut further into my schooling. In our family, out of necessity, working on the farm had to take precedent over education. But even when I was six or seven, I would get up ridiculously early to work in the fields and finish all my chores so that I could go to school.

My first school was a one-room building known as Pleasant Grove. It was heated by a wood-burning stove in the middle of the room. When it got cold, all the students would huddle around the stove to keep warm. With all the pushing and shoving, I sustained a nasty burn when I was forced up against it.

The stove wasn't the worst of my experiences, however.

Every day, I would get up at 4:00, and do my best to get all my work done so I could walk to school at 7:00, Occasionally, because of all my chores, I would be late to school. In those instances, I was given a whipping by the teacher. These days, that would be considered child abuse, but back then it was the norm.

On top of that, on the way to school, I had to walk past the home of a family that was loaded with bullies…boys who took special delight in being mean to anyone and everything. Most of us kids decided that our best option was to race past this house as fast as we could. I decided, though, that I'd try to be brave and walk at a normal pace, but fear would overtake me and I'd break into a run. That skill would serve me well during my "track and field" days later on, but at that moment, all I cared about was avoiding certain conflict.

The bottom line? Getting an education was not the most painless thing back in those days! But education was important enough to me that I was willing to put up with all of the challenges.

But there is another "bottom line" that impacts families today, whether they be Black families, White families, Hispanic families, or families of any other heritage.

Today, most kids are raised without the presence or active involvement of two parents—both a mother and a father. I was blessed by the fact that both my mother and father were concerned about my present life and my future life. They loved me, they nurtured me, they prayed for me, they had dreams for me. They didn't let poverty, or racism, or any other circumstances dictate the person I instinctively knew that I wanted to become.

I've discovered that life comes to us in "bursts" – revelations that come to us over time – always at the right time. We don't know everything when we are born. We don't know everything at age 5. We do not fully grasp life at age 12, or 15, or 18, or 25. Learning about life is a beautiful, long-term process. It begins at birth and ends only when we die.

It's so sad to read the statistics about kids who don't experience the loving involvement of two parents, or of supportive siblings, or of loving grandparents.

As vital as "book learning" is, "Life Learning" and "Love Learning" top the list of what every kid needs.

Rosey's Rose-Colored Gem

We all learn from a variety of sources and experiences...not just school...not simply books. Among our "teachers" are our parents, our siblings, our friends, our role models, the media, and popular entertainment. One of the great secrets in life is to learn to discriminate among all the competing voices in order to learn those things that really matter.

Chapter Three

Moving Toward the Future

"Let others lead small lives, but not you.
Let others argue over small things, but not you.
Let others cry over small hurts, but not you.
Let others leave their future in someone else's hands, but not you."

—Jim Rohn

It was called the "Chicken Trail." It got its name from a train that ran north from Georgia to what was called "Yankee Territory." "Yankee" had nothing to do with the baseball team. It basically just meant, "North of the Mason-Dixon Line."

When I was about eight, my mother's sister, Aunt Lulabelle, who lived in New Jersey, contacted my dad and said, "Y'all gotta move outta Georgia. Where are you going with your life, anyway? You plow and you plant and you harvest, and you don't make any money. We just bought a house and y'all can come live with us."

One of Aunt Lulabelle's "selling points" was, "You can get a good job up here." The other one was, "Your children need a good school. They need a better education."

Dad thought it over, and decided. One night over dinner, he announced to the family, "We're going to move up north, but don't tell anyone about it."

Of course, I blabbed it to everyone.

Poppa was furious. "I told you not to tell anyone, now everyone is asking me about it." As the result of my indiscretion, I received one big whooping… that was his way of dealing with me.

Dad traveled to New Jersey first…to look for a job, and to become comfortable with the idea of uprooting the family and moving to another state.

By that time in my life—age nine—I was the oldest boy in the house…the others had gotten married and moved away.

Some of my sisters had left, too. My older sister, Eula, married a man named King Blackwell, whose family was pretty well off. They all had cars—a big thing back then—while we just had a wagon and a mule. When King returned from military service, his head was all bashed and bandaged. But that wasn't the result of war injuries. He and some other Black servicemen were stopped by the police in some Southern town.

"I'm just bettin' you boys have some pictures of some White girls in your wallets," one of the officers said.

Sure enough, one of them was carrying a picture of a White girl from overseas. The police pulled them out of the car and beat them all violently. My brother-in-law was badly injured.

Despite the fact that I was angry about this incident, I still somehow saw it as "isolated." I didn't know that all of this represented the general attitude in the South. It wasn't until our family moved North that this reality began to dawn on me. But, the truth was, things weren't that much better in New Jersey…as I would eventually discover.

As the oldest boy left at home, I was forced to assume a lot of "adult roles" very quickly. My dad instructed me to sell all of the farm equipment and furniture while he was gone, so that we could lighten our load for our trip.

Fortunately for me, my parents supported the idea of a better education for their younger children. I guess they thought that our future was worth the move.

We boarded the train one day with all the worldly possessions we could pack and carry, along with a huge tub of homemade fried chicken. Everyone on the train carried a similar bucket of fried chicken, and as we ate on our journey, we would all throw the bones out the window. That, as I'm sure you've guessed by now, is where the "Chicken Trail" designation came from.

The move was both exciting and terrifying to me, but the train ride itself was quite a revelation. For one thing, I was getting some idea about how big our country is. I was also seeing how people lived. Some lived in shacks. Some lived in big fancy houses. Some lived on tiny lots in big cities, crammed together so tightly I wondered how they were able to move. Others lived on expansive farms of rolling land, acres and acres of crops, and huge barns and silos. I was just beginning to understand the cultural, economic, and racial diversity of America.

The things I witnessed on that trip were unbelievable. Passing through Atlanta, I saw a car high up in a huge tree. I figured out that it was some kind of advertisement. It was the most incredible thing I had ever seen in my life.

We finally arrived in Roselle, New Jersey, and settled into Aunt Lulabelle's comfortable home.

If you're thinking *It must have been major culture shock for young Rosey to move from a small town in Georgia to New Jersey*, you're right. Young Rosey was culturally shocked.

For the first time in my life, I went to school with White kids. My school in Georgia was 100% Black.

As a result of my life in Georgia, I didn't know anything about White kids. Yes, there was one family of white kids that we knew in Cuthbert. They would come over and eat dinner with us occasionally…and we would go to their place and eat with them. At the age of seven, I was told by the White family to add "Mr." or "Miss" to the beginning of their children's names, which made a class distinction. But they were poor, as were we, so they didn't seem all that different. On the other hand, some of the kids in New Jersey had money. Not "big" money, but more money than I had ever seen.

Money seemed to be a divisive factor among people back then, and the issue is still with us today.

Another shock—or more of a pleasant surprise—in Georgia I was only able to attend school three days a week, because of my responsibilities on the farm. In New Jersey, I was able to go to classes five days a week.

But that pleasant surprise was followed by an unpleasant one. As much as I loved school, I was terribly far behind. Thankfully for my self-esteem, I was placed at my grade level—fifth grade—even though it was a struggle for me.

I was able to catch up, mostly because of a new friend named John Grossi. He was an Italian kid who was getting straight A's. He didn't take my tests for me. He didn't cheat. What he did was he changed my attitude. I had self-doubts. He taught me about the fundamentals. He showed me that the key was getting to the basic core of the problem, because then it would no longer be a problem.

I eventually discovered that this is true in school, it's true in football, and it's true in life. Work hard on solving the fundamentals!

Shortly after we arrived in New Jersey, I met some cousins I didn't know about. They lived in Linden. I soon learned that most kids my age who lived in Linden didn't like kids who lived in Roselle. But I could "cross the border" because my cousins lived there, and the bullies wouldn't bother me. It didn't hurt that I was bigger than most of them. In fact, I'd say it helped!

My best childhood friend was a guy named John Arthur Wilson, who moved to New Jersey about the same time we did.

One day, John told me that he was going to quit school. I tried to talk him out of it. "Man, you need to go to school. That's the only way to have a future."

He laughed and said, "Well, Rosey, when you graduate, you can come work for me."

John's dad sold firewood, and he would drive around various neighborhoods offering it door-to-door. Sometimes I got to work on the truck with him. I learned to work together with other kids who didn't especially like us. John never finished school, but he has been a success in life, and we are still friends to this day.

I developed several new interests in junior high and high school—besides girls, of course.

I became interested in singing; I was a part of a "Spiritual/Gospel" quartet, and I also sang in the glee club. Yes, that kind of "TV Glee Club."

In ninth grade, I got into organized sports. I was tall, so I tried basketball. But I was no future Kobe Bryant or LeBron James. I could barely catch the ball, let alone shoot it. But if they had needed a big guy to knock the other players over, I would have been their guy. They didn't need that.

However, because I was big and muscular, my sport of choice (and natural ability) was track and field. My specialties were shot put, discus, javelin, and long jump. Plus, I was a sprinter. These skills and abilities served me well. I was named to the "All-State" team, and my records much later helped me get into my college of choice—Penn State—with an athletic scholarship.

But at about the same time in New Jersey, I also discovered a strange game that involved a big grassy field with stripes on it, using a strange-shaped ball that could be thrown straight as an arrow, or it could hit the ground and bounce wildly and unpredictably. Yes, in New Jersey, I found a game that a lot of top athletes played. It's called football.

The coach saw me in the hall, and asked me if I would like to play with the big boys. I said, "Of course, yes!" So he invited me to come down to the football field. I went down to the field with my books in my hand and stood by the sidelines watching them practice. An assistant coach asked me to come to the locker room with him and get a uniform. I laid my books and glasses on the ground at the edge of the field and followed the coach to the locker room. I put on my uniform and came back out and joined the players. They told me what to do, because I had never played football before.

However, they had 'played over' the area where I had put my books and glasses. They had been playing at the other end of the field, and when I put my books and glasses down, I had no idea how long the playing field was. When we got to that end of the field, I saw my books and glasses all scrambled. I immediately wanted to know, "Who did this?" The coaches then let me know that was part of the playing field, and they would replace my glasses and books. (Without them replacing them, I would not be able to purchase new ones.}

The game seemed to be fun, and the rules appeared to me to be fairly simple.

The team on defense kicks off the ball…the offense grabs it and tries to run the ball to the goal on the other end of the field to score a touchdown.

If they don't make it all the way, the offense tries to get "first downs." They try to move the ball at least ten yards forward in four tries. If they make it ten yards or more, they get another four tries to move the ball at least another ten yards…another first down.

So the quarterback may decide to try running plays or passing plays. In a passing play, he throws the ball to a designated receiver. The defense tries to stop him before he makes a first down or scores a touchdown.

When the other team has the ball, that means you're on defense, and your goal was to stop them from scoring a touchdown…by ramming into them as hard as you could, piling on them, and hopefully even taking the ball away from them.

When I started playing football, I was tried out on both offense and defense.

When my team was on offense and I had the ball, I wasn't the easiest guy to bring down. And when the other team had the ball, I would knock the stuffing out of whatever kid had it. I soon took this game seriously.

Throughout high school, I got written up in the local newspaper on a regular basis. But no one outside of the reporters or my coach seemed to care. My dad didn't care. My mom didn't care. My cousins didn't care. Aunt Lulabelle didn't care.

They were never at my games. They always had something else to do.

I'd come home after school, and they'd ask, "Well, what did you do today?"

"Oh, we had a football game," I'd say.

"How'd you do?"

"We won."

But they never asked me about the game. In my family, it was considered bad manners to brag about your accomplishments. My parents taught me that. So I didn't.

Fortunately, I've never been the kind of person who is easily discouraged by circumstances. Ultimately, football became my game. And my game plan. My future.

Rosey's Rose-Colored Gem

Some people believe that, for the most part, the future is something that just "happens" to you. Yes, some things that impact your life are inevitable, and you really don't have control over them. But if you learn how to analyze situations, choose the best options, apply wisdom, and take action with enthusiasm and energy, you will be more in charge of your future than you ever imagined possible!

Chapter Four

Dreaming Big

"Football is like life—it requires perseverance, self-denial, hard work, sacrifice, dedication and respect for authority."

—Vince Lombardi (Legendary Coach of the *Green Bay Packers*)

I imagine that every high school football player's dream is to get recruited by a top college team. And every successful college player's dream is to get drafted by a winning NFL team. Naturally, then, every professional football player's dream is to play in the Super Bowl and wear that 12-pound gold championship ring every day for the rest of his life.

I wasn't born with the dream. But it grew in me over the years. In time, I realized that I just might have the talent. I knew I had the focus and the drive.

But I began my football career in a time very different from today. I endured scorn and ridicule and derision because I didn't fit the picture of an "ideal" player. I wasn't White.

Now, please know that I'm not going to whine and moan and "play the race card" here. It was simply the way things were. At the time, I didn't know they would change. I hoped they would, but it sure didn't look that way.

High school wasn't all that racially confrontational. I felt that I was accepted despite my color.

I invested much of my time and energy in sports, and I was rewarded for my efforts. I was named "All American" in track, "All State" in football, and even "All County" in basketball. (As I told you, I entered the world of football quite by accident.)

Then along came the opportunity for college. I lived one of those dream stories where college recruiters would come to my door and invite me to tour their campuses.

The first school I visited was Virginia State. I fell in love with that school, only because I laid eyes on a blue-eyed Black girl. I had never seen such captivating beauty before that day.

When I got home from school one day, I was greeted with big news from my dad. He said that a coach from Penn State named Norm Gordon had come to see me. Coach Gordon promised to remunerate me if I paid my own way to come visit them. I didn't understand the concept of remuneration at the time, but I eagerly boarded a bus to travel to State College, Pennsylvania, the borough that serves as home to the main campus of that large university.

I was impressed, even though I didn't spot any blue-eyed Black girls on campus. The thing I liked about Penn State is that they didn't talk about football. They talked about academics…about graduating. They talked about learning skills and entering a serious profession.

I was offered a track scholarship, which I accepted, even though my primary interest was football. By going with the track scholarship, a football scholarship opened up for another player they were recruiting.

Back in high school, I never took college preparatory courses. Most teachers tried to talk Black kids into taking non-college prep classes, so I followed their advice. Despite that fact, I still passed my courses at Penn State, though near the bottom of my class. I eventually earned a Bachelor of Science degree in Physical Education, with a minor in Psychology.

I decided that one of my non-sports pursuits should be music, since I enjoyed singing. But I had no serious musical background, and I didn't know how to read music. So what did they do? They handed me a cello and said, "Here, learn to play this."

Well, they might have well have handed me a kid's chemistry set and said, "Here, Roosevelt, build a rocket and go to the moon." So I changed my major to Physical Education.

The other students were extremely helpful and they tried to help me catch up. It didn't matter: I was about to flunk out—which would make me ineligible for track season. It took a lot of hard work—consistent work—to earn passing grades and stay in school. I very quickly learned that Dreams + Desire + Persistence = Success.

I wasn't permitted to play football during my freshman year. When I finally got to play, the other players really tested me. One guy dove at me hard and hit me on my chin knocking me to the ground. Hey, that's football! I got so energized—so mad, really—that no one could keep up with me after that incident. I started in the next game and I played both offense and defense throughout college. In fact, I never lost my starting position until I retired from professional football. Desire and persistence really pay off!

Playing at Penn State was where I also got a major "wake-up" call: Racism was alive and well, even in the North. Remember, this is years before Dr. Martin Luther King, Jr. and the Civil Rights Movement.

I discovered that no matter how good the Black players were, the coaches would never allow more than five of us on the field at the same time.

Not only that, but on one road trip to play another team, we tried to check into a motel and were told that Black players were not permitted to stay there. We were forced to stay at a different motel. My coach was as supportive as he could be, but it didn't matter to the motel owner.

For the most part, all that is in the past. College and NFL players are recruited and put on the field based on their abilities. There are no more race quotas. So yes, that's why you see so many talented Blacks in football at every level. Same thing in basketball. But not so much in baseball or hockey. I can't quite figure that one out!

Now that "equal *play* for equal work" issue is resolved, all that remains is to eradicate the rest of the deep-rooted racism that often boils under the surface. Not very long ago, the owner of the Los Angeles Clippers reminded us all of that reality. He paid a huge price for the thoughts he had boiling inside his mind and heart.

The good thing, I think, is that my opinions and attitudes don't have to be shaped by someone else's. Just because another person harbors negative thoughts or feelings about me doesn't mean I have to accept them. And just because someone believes that I do not have a right to my dreams doesn't mean that I can't pursue my dreams with desire and persistence—and faith.

My simple advice would be, "Live Your Dream, and Live Your Life. No one has the right to stop you!"

Rosey's Rose-Colored Gem

We aren't born with the innate ability to dream big dreams for our lives. We have to either learn how to dream on our own, or we have to allow ourselves to be inspired or encouraged by others.

Chapter Five

The World of Football: Then Versus Now

"Progress is a nice word. But change is its motivator. And change has its enemies."

—Robert Kennedy

Many of my friends—and even my own family—have observed that I don't talk…whine…complain a lot about racism.

Have I seen it? Yes.

Have I been the victim of it to some extent? Yes.

Did I understand it? Well, a little bit.

Think about it. Here was this new country cropping up out of nowhere. The United States of America. Growing. Expanding. People from Europe exploring their new home. Mostly White, many of them wealthy—or at least wealthy enough to buy, build, or board a ship and travel to a new continent. It was a huge land-mass populated by—in their minds at the time—a few insignificant natives.

But it didn't take long for the "New Americans" to discover that they couldn't achieve all of their "New American Dreams" without a little outside help. Thanks to the lessons many of them learned from their British forbearers, they knew that all the help they needed could be imported directly from Africa—on ships loaded with African natives.

My ancestors were on those ships. But as a young kid, I had no clue. Growing up in rural Georgia, I knew little about slavery. I didn't get much of a glimpse of racism. Those relatives were in the past. I was in the present. Yes, it was the 1930s and 1940s. But that was "the Present" for me.

My family was Black. My neighbors were Black. My schoolmates were Black. My church was Black. And my "Present" was 100% Black. It worked for me...because I didn't know anything different.

My eyes had been partially opened when I got to Penn State. But they were further opened when I became part of the NFL—the National Football League.

When you watch a professional football game today—either in the stands in the stadium or on television—you probably don't spend a lot of time (if any) thinking about the racial/ethnic backgrounds of the players on the field. You just want your favorite team to win, make it to the playoffs, and win the Super Bowl.

But it hasn't always been that way. When I played with the New York Giants back in the late 1950's, something called the "quota system" was in place. That meant there were positions for only six Blacks on the Giants team. Most NFL teams adhered to that system. Some teams, including the Washington Redskins, didn't allow *any* Black players. (For me, this form of discrimination had begun in college, and it continued in pro football.)

Most of the Black players at the time played on the offensive and defensive lines. Those positions were considered rough, tough, and dirty. I don't recall any Black players in those days who played the positions of center, quarterback, or linebacker. Whites were thought to be more educated and better able to make crucial decisions and call plays.

I considered myself to have been blessed. Coming out of the football program at Penn State University, I was drafted as the 31st overall pick in the third round of the 1955 NFL Draft by the Los Angeles Rams. But I was traded to the New York Giants before I played my first season. Yet, I felt that I was doing quite well for a Georgia boy, by way of New Jersey and Pennsylvania.

I played with the Giants from 1955 to 1962. Our team won the NFL Championship in 1956, and the Eastern Conference Championship in 1958, 1959, 1961 and 1962. I was also selected for the Pro Bowl in 1956, and I was named All-Pro at the defensive tackle position for several of those years.

This was, however, the era in America when, if the Army came calling, we young guys answered. Elvis Presley answered, joining the Army in 1958. Two years into my career with the Giants, I was drafted into the Army.

I wasn't as famous as Elvis was when he joined, but some people knew about my Penn State days and recognized me from my short career with the Giants. So, as you might expect, I was asked to play football for the Army.

That was not my goal, however. I didn't want to play football with the Army. I wanted to go home on weekends and play with the Giants.

At about that time, the military changed their policy, and pro football players could no longer be in the Army and play football at the same time.

They offered me a choice: play Army football or become a foot soldier. So, I played Army football.

In my first game, I felt I was being punished for something or other, because I played on the fourth team. But by the end of the game, I was leading the team in defense. In fact, we won 10 games in a row that year.

I played in the "All-Army Game." We lost that one. In my opinion, it was because so many guys on our team were drinking and partying the night before the game. Anyone who doesn't think he needs to be sober, wide awake, and alert before playing in a big game—or any game—is just kidding himself.

When we played a game in North Carolina, we Black players discovered that we couldn't go to any of the nightclubs. Our only choice was to go to "back door" clubs—seedy dives that usually invited trouble. That didn't appeal to me, so I just stayed in my room.

When I would get a pass, I would go home to New Jersey on the bus to see my family. Remember, this was the South, before Rosa Parks, so I was told where to sit. "Hey, you! You can't sit there. Sit in the back."

As a big guy, I filled up the seat, and my knees touched the back of the seat in front of me. Naturally, the White guy in front of me decided to recline his seat as far as it would go, crushing my knees and jamming me into my seat.

"Sir, could you please pull your seat upright?" I asked politely.

"Nope. Not gonna happen," he muttered.

I sat there immobilized and in pain for hundreds of miles. I couldn't get him to get his seat off my legs until we crossed the

Mason Dixon Line. Then, almost as if by magic, he started playing by the game by the slightly more progressive "Rules of the North." He brought his chair upright. I wanted to say, "thank you," but I thought the better of it. I didn't need that kind of engagement.

During this time, I met a White family who befriended and frequently invited me over for dinner. My relationship with them taught me a valuable lesson: Don't judge an entire race based on the rude behavior of one miserable man on a bus!

I went home to see my family as often as I could (the bus incident never happened again). When I was away from home, I missed my family, but when I was home, I missed my Giants teammates.

Yes, I knew I had to fulfill my duty. But while I believe it is our responsibility as Americans to serve our country, I couldn't wait to get discharged from the Army and get back to playing the game I loved.

I truly valued playing in New York. Not only was it close to home, but our defensive line was called "The FRONT FOUR." The line consisted of Andy Robustelli, Dick Modzelewski, Jim Katcavage, and myself. We had the best defensive line in football. Tom Landry came up with a new defensive system called the "4-3." I was also playing with great teammates including Frank Gifford, Y.A. Tittle, Sam Huff, Rosie Brown, Kyle Rote, and Emlin Tunnell. We had great coaches as well—among them head coach

Jim Howell, offensive coach Vince Lombardi, and defensive coach Tom Landry. Can you imagine what we players learned from those guys? The players are Hall of Famers and so are Tom Landry and Vince Lombardi.

From 1958 to 1963, we played in the NFL Championship Game five times. But, sadly, we won only one of them. Among the most memorable and disappointing of those games was our 1958 NFL Championship Game against the Baltimore Colts. We lost in overtime 23–17, yet it is often referred to as "The Greatest Game Ever Played" and it really helped professional football gain in stature with fans.

The following year, we lost the championship to the Colts again, giving up a 16–9 4th quarter lead to suffer a 31–16 loss. In 1963, led by league MVP quarterback Y.A. Tittle, the Giants again played in the NFL Championship Game, where they lost to the Chicago Bears 14 to 10. But I did not play in that game. I had been traded to the Los Angeles Rams.

Quite naturally, I was disappointed when I was sent to the Rams in July, 1962, in exchange for a defensive tackle and a high future draft pick.

Despite all of the losses in the "big games," I still had the sense that I was always playing with winners. I had left behind a championship-level team to join what I thought was a weak franchise.

My frustration was short-lived, though. I ultimately became part of a defensive line that included Lamar Lundy, Deacon Jones, and Merlin Olsen.

Lamar J. Lundy, Jr. joined the Rams as defensive end in 1957, and played for the same team until 1969—13 seasons. Because he was tall (6'7"), he was drafted by both the NBA and the NFL. He came out of Purdue University, where he was the first Black student to receive a football scholarship. In fact, he was named MVP of both the football and basketball teams in his senior year. Quite an achievement!

Deacon Jones was the next to join the Rams. He was drafted in the 14th round of the 1961 NFL Draft. He quickly earned a starting role as a defensive end. If you're a football fan, you've undoubtedly heard the term "Sacking the Quarterback." That was Deacon's original term for what he did. It has since been adopted throughout football. If there had been official records of "sacks" kept back then, Deacon would probably still be the record-holder. Deacon was traded to the San Diego Chargers in 1972, and ended his career with the Washington Redskins in 1974. In his very last game, the Redskins allowed him to kick the point-after-touchdown for the game's last score!

Merlin Olsen played professional football from 1962 to 1976—the entire time for the Rams. He was a very intense, consistent, dependable player, and missed only two games in 15 seasons. He was selected as the NFL's Rookie of the Year in 1962, and named All-Pro for several years. Merlin was also one of the better-paid players of our era. His first contract was for around $50,000 for two years, plus a signing bonus. The average salary for a professional football player in 1962 was about $12,000 a year. Not much compared to today, that's for sure!

I was the last of the four to join "the line." The group.

When I met these three guys, I immediately knew that I would be playing with "giants," even though they were not New York Giants! We became friends, and we became the defensive line of the L.A. Rams.

For those of you who are not all that into football, that meant that we were the four guys up front, hands in the dirt, facing the other team, and our job was to crash through the opponent's offensive line (generally consisting of four other big guys), chase down their quarterback and get to whomever had the ball. Our job was to stop "forward progress" and hopefully get the ball back. As the saying goes, "It was an ugly job, but someone had to do it." And the more we did it, the better we got at it.

We became an extremely cohesive group of four intense guys who wanted to be the best at what we did. For our efforts, we became known as the "Fearsome Foursome." And trust me when I tell you that we were truly feared.

I realize that football is a violent game, and players can get seriously injured. But that is not the object of the game. (And if an injury is serious, the announcers tell viewers to turn their heads.) Still, some of you may prefer baseball, or golf, or chess.

That's fine. But to get you "back onto my page," I have to tell you that Lamar, Merlin, and Deacon—off the field—were probably the gentlest, kindest, most non-violent guys you could ever meet. We played a game. We had fun. We were paid for it. We weren't paid much by today's standards, but we got money for playing the game. We loved it!

After we retired from football, all of us got involved in acting. Merlin was the busiest of all of us. If you are old enough, you might remember that he played the role of a farmer, Jonathan Garvey, on *LITTLE HOUSE ON THE PRAIRIE*, the popular series starring Michael Landon. After that, he starred in his own show on NBC, *FATHER MURPHY*.

Lamar was less involved in acting, but he appeared in the un-aired pilot for *LOST IN SPACE*. It eventually aired as Episode 4 of the series: "There Were Giants in the Earth." That fit, because

Lamar was one of the giants of the Rams! After he retired from playing he became an assistant coach for the San Diego Chargers.

Deacon Jones worked as a television actor, and appeared in numerous TV programs since the 1970s, most often appearing in cameo roles. He appeared in an episode of *THE ODD COUPLE* in which he and Oscar were in a television commercial selling shaving products. He appeared on *THE BRADY BUNCH*, and on *BEWITCHED*, and he even played himself in an episode of *WONDER WOMAN* in 1978.

I enjoyed venturing into music and acting, as well, and I'll be telling you more about that later on.

All of us also got involved in various charities and community endeavors.

Lamar's love was kids—his own kids and others. He often returned to his hometown of Richmond, Indiana, to get involved in various community projects and youth events. He'd invite the rest of us in the "Foursome" to help out, and we did. Near the end of his life, Lamar returned to Richmond full-time. As sick as he was, he would go down to the Townsend Community Center and helped neighborhood kids with their homework or introduce them to basketball. Most of these kids lived with working single parents, so he fulfilled an important role in their lives. I can only imagine how many of these kids will find success in life because Lamar cared.

Merlin also loved kids and often served as the co-host for the Children's Miracle Network telethons. CMN was founded in 1983 by Marie Osmond and John Schneider to raise funds for children's hospitals and medical research.

Deacon served as the president and CEO of the Deacon Jones Foundation, an organization he founded in 1997 "to assist young people and the communities in which they live with a comprehensive program that includes education, mentoring, corporate internship, and community service." He also made several trips to visit the U. S. military in Iraq.

My charitable endeavors have largely involved work with street gangs and the elderly—two forgotten groups. I'll discuss that in a later chapter. Sadly, I am the only still-living member of the "Fearsome Foursome."

Lamar Lundy, who battled diabetes, cancer, and heart disease, died at age 71 on February 24, 2007. Merlin Olsen died of cancer at age 69 on March 11, 2010, at City of Hope National Medical Center in Duarte, California. Deacon Jones died at age 74 of natural causes at his home in Anaheim Hills, California. June 3, 2013.

Football has changed a lot since my playing days. For one thing, the LA Rams became the St. Louis Rams in 1994, a fact that really bothered Deacon. He campaigned actively for a new team in LA and a new stadium. He insisted that the St. Louis Rams adopt a different name, also. He did not see his dreams fulfilled in his lifetime. In 2016, the Rams came home to LA and are building a new stadium. There is a rumor that there may be a statue of the "Fearsome Foursome" at the new stadium, also.

Another big change: there were no multi-million dollar contracts back then. I think we played more for the love of the game than for money. Today, top NFL players can demand multi-year contracts in the millions.

According to Forbes Magazine (Forbes.com), Drew Brees, quarterback for the New Orleans Saints, earned approximately $51 million dollars in 2013—$40 million from salary and bonuses, and $11 million from product endorsements. If he had earned an equivalent amount in 1963, based on the rate of inflation, he still would have made more than $6.58 million. Trust me, I didn't make anything close to that. Of course, I wasn't the Drew Brees of my era, either. But NO player was paid anything close to that when I played.

Finally, the "quota system" that existed when I started my NFL career has obviously gone away for good. As I noted earlier, back then, there could not be more than 6 Black players on any team's roster. Today, close to 70% of all NFL players are African-American.

But for years—if not decades—Blacks were not known to play the position of quarterback in the NFL—or even in college football. The reason was that Blacks were perceived as not smart enough to run the offense. They had "fast legs," but not strong arms or quick minds. (Of course, the same was said for the great Johnny Unitas, who played for the Baltimore Colts when they defeated us Giants 23–17 in sudden death overtime in the December 28, 1958, NFL championship game.)

Time and on-the-field performance have dispelled the false notion about Black quarterbacks.

Randall Cunningham led the NFL in passing rating (a combination of factors) in 1988, when he played for the Philadelphia Eagles, the team he remained with through the 1995 season. He later played for the Minnesota Vikings (1997–1999), the Dallas Cowboys (2000), and the Baltimore Ravens (2001). Cunningham then rejoined the Philadelphia Eagles and ultimately retired in 2002.

Warren Moon played for the Houston Oilers, Minnesota Vikings, Seattle Seahawks, and Kansas City Chiefs. He held the record for most passing touchdowns and the most pass completions in professional football until his record was eventually surpassed by Brett Favre. He was named to the Pro Football Hall of Fame in 2006.

Doug Williams was the quarterback for the Washington Redskins and led his team to a lopsided victory (42-10) over the Denver Broncos in Super Bowl XXII. (John Elway was his quarterback opponent.) Doug passed for a Super Bowl record of 340 yards and four touchdowns, with one interception. He was the first player in Super Bowl history to pass for four touchdowns in a single quarter, and four in a half. Doug Williams was the first black starting quarterback to win a Super Bowl, and he was named the MVP of that game.

Russell Wilson of the Seattle Seahawks was the second Black quarterback to lead his team to victory in a Super Bowl. Wilson threw for 206 yards, two touchdowns, and no interceptions in the 43-8 defeat over the Denver Broncos in 2014. He played college football for the University of Wisconsin during the 2011 season, and led the team to a Big Ten title and the 2012 Rose Bowl. Not only did Russell Wilson lead the Seahawks to their first Super Bowl win in the team's 38-year history, but he also became the second Black starting quarterback to win a Super Bowl, joining Doug Williams.

Someday, somewhere, someone is going to read this book, and come to this realization: "I've been told all my life that I'm not smart enough, fast enough, big enough, talented enough, musical enough, or 'whatever' enough to achieve my dreams. I choose to refuse that. I will not believe those thoughts about myself, whether they are my own, or they are pushed into my mind by others. I will be a Russell Wilson or a Doug Williams, or a Warren Moon, or a Randall Cunningham!"

Rosey's Rose-Colored Gem

I've heard many people complain, "I was just born at the wrong time. If only I had lived in the (Decade and Century), I could have (Accomplished This or That).

Well, I was born in the right at the right time, in the right place, to the right family, for all the right reasons. I have always believed that, and those beliefs have always served me well.

Chapter Six

Everyone Needs
A Hobby

"Make the most of today. Get interested in something.
Shake yourself awake.
Develop a hobby.
Let the winds of enthusiasm sweep through you.
Live today with gusto."

—Dale Carnegie

I realize that many people think of football as "merely a game." And, in the NFL, those people think of it as a highly-paid game. (Not so much the case in my era, as I explained.)

But football is actually a very stressful game. Every time I walked out on the field, I knew that my job was to crash into another big player who was on the offense in order to get through to the quarterback or whoever had the ball—and stop forward progress. And I knew that the job of offensive player on the other side of the line of scrimmage was to crash into me as hard as he could, to keep me from getting through to the ball carrier.

What we had here was two big players—I was 6'5" and weighed about 284 pounds when I played in the NFL, and the players I faced were usually about the same size—who were willing to hurt each other…and get hurt…to make the big plays and win games.

I don't know what most people would call that situation, but I'd call it stress. And if I got caught grabbing a facemask, I'd draw a penalty for my team, and my next appearance in the locker room would not be pleasant. More stress.

So, I decided that maybe I needed some sort of hobby to help settle my nerves and take my mind off the next time I was about to get hit by a big player on the offense. I just had no idea what that hobby would be.

It wasn't until after I retired from football that I stumbled upon a perfect hobby. Perfect for me, anyway. I was on the Phil Donahue show on TV as one of his guests, and he was interviewing Sylvia Sydney, who was extolling the virtues of needlepoint. She had me attempting to do needlepoint on the show. The audience was really amused. After the show, I really didn't give needlepoint another thought.

In the course of my daily activities, I would often drive down Wilshire Boulevard. Like most commuters, when I came to a stoplight, I would sit in my car and glance around at my surroundings. At one particular intersection, I noticed that the surroundings were particularly pleasant. Beautiful, I'd have to say.

There was a store near that intersection, and I observed that several very attractive women were entering and leaving that store. I have always appreciated attractive women (I was a guy, after all! And at that time, I was a single guy.) So I just HAD to know what was going on in there.

One day, I had some extra time, so I pulled over, parked, and with my guitar over my back, I walked in. It turned out that the store sold supplies for needlepoint. I knew absolutely nothing about needlepoint, other than what Sylvia had shown me, so I found a woman in the store and started asking her questions. I even boldly volunteered to give her advice on needlepoint.

When she told me that she found it relaxing (she called it a "tension buster"), I knew I might have found my new diversion.

The owner of the shop came over to me and said, "Rosey, if you are going to come in the shop and tell the ladies what they're doing wrong, maybe you should take lessons first." I agreed and started to take lessons.

My first efforts were simple enough, but extremely crudely done. I didn't show them to anyone, because I knew I would be embarrassed.

Over time, I became more skilled and more confident, so I decided I could possibly do needlepoint when I went on trips by airplane.

I was terrified of flying! In my non-technical mind, there was no logical reason why a long, people-filled metal tube with wings could fly at 400 or 500 miles an hour, 25,0000, 30,000 feet or more above the earth, and feel safe.

I recalled what the attractive lady at the craft store had told me about needlepoint: "It's a tension buster. It will help you relax."

So I brought my little "kit" on my next flight, and I got to work on a project. I also got strange looks from the passengers seated next to me. And the passengers on their way to the bathroom. And the flight attendants.

Thinking about it now, it must have been a fairly comical sight. A big, bearded Black guy sitting in his seat doing a "woman's thing." Over time, some passengers who recognized me would comment. I would describe these folks as "curious, but kind."

It's probably a good idea that I didn't discover the relaxing benefits of needlepoint when I was playing football for Penn State, or the New York Giants, or the Los Angeles Rams. I can't begin to imagine the heckling I have been forced to endure. Merlin would have been merciless. Deacon would have joined right in.

Thankfully, Lamar was the quiet one, so he probably would have just laughed on the inside.

This genteel activity actually gained me a bit of notoriety. Enough, in fact, that I was asked to author a "picture book" about my hobby. It was titled *NEEDLEPOINT FOR MEN*, and it was published in 1973. In November of 1974, my needlepoint work was featured on the cover of the *SATURDAY EVENING POST*.

These days, the only place you might be able to catch a glimpse of me engaged in my hobby is on YouTube, in a television spot for the Prostate Cancer Foundation. Its cause is very important to me. (More on that later.)

Just go to YouTube.com and search for "Rosey Grier Prostate Cancer." This link may also still be active: http://www.youtube.com/watch?v=6Hvr5FbpgmM

As important as my hobby was to me at the time I took it up, I believe that the humor inherent in my little pursuit has helped a lot of people since that time. And giving back to our communities and our world is a significant part of "balance."

Rosey's Rose-Colored Gem

Life can't be all about one thing. It can't be all about work. It can't be all about food…or pleasure…or hobbies.

Balance is the key, I believe.

Chapter Seven

Anybody Here Seen My Good Friend, Bobby?

"But suppose God is black? What if we go to Heaven and we, all our lives, have treated the Negro as an inferior, and God is there, and we look up and

He is not white? What then is our response?"

—Robert Kennedy

Dion DiMucci, the pop star of the 50s and 60s (whom I have never met) recorded a poignant song in 1968: "Abraham, Martin, and John." It became a hit, due, I believe, to Dion's performance combined with the emotional subject matter of the lyrics.

It was a song about three Americans who had lost their lives fighting for freedom for all of us. Not on a battlefield somewhere half way around the world, but here at home—simply because they believed they could make a difference.

Abraham Lincoln lost his life as the result of a gunshot wound in the Ford Theatre in Washington, D.C. He was a fighter, a champion of freedom, a man whose high principles led the nation into a long, ugly, Civil War. There simply was no other way to fight that fight.

President John F. Kennedy is the "John" in the song. He reignited the spirit of America with his youthful energy and lofty sense of purpose and renewal. He, too, was struck down by an assassin's bullets, while he rode down the streets of Dallas, Texas, in an open limousine, his wife at his side.

"Martin" is Dr. Martin Luther King, Jr., the pre-eminent voice for civil rights in the twentieth century. One ugly, tragic day in Memphis, the voice of the man who uttered the words "I have a dream…" was silenced. The voice died, but his ideas and ideals live on.

Then, in Dion's song, a final name surfaced. "Anybody here seen my old friend Bobby? Can you tell me where he's gone? I thought I saw him walkin' up over the hill, with Abraham, Martin, and John."

I knew Robert F. "Bobby" Kennedy. But not for as long as I had hoped.

For the second time in my life, I watched a man die. A good man. A decent man. A man who cared about you, about me, and about every other person in America—if not the world. The day he died, my Rosey-colored glasses were nowhere to be found. It was a dark day for me.

When my football career with the L.A. Rams ended in 1966 as the result of an injury, I was lost in a sea of purposelessness. I was looking for a place, a position, a role—something where I could make a difference. I wanted to use whatever skills, connections, and so-called "fame" I had to impact society. I had been given so much, I thought. It was time to give back. In 1968, I decided to become involved in the presidential campaign of Senator Robert F. Kennedy, a man affectionately known as "Bobby." But originally, it wasn't my idea. It was someone else's.

You may remember, or may have read, that the year 1968 was not a good one for Black People. In retrospect, many White people would agree that it wasn't a good year for them, either.

The Reverend Martin Luther King, Jr. had emerged on the American scene several years earlier as a significant voice for civil rights. He was known for his eloquent speaking style as well as his commitment to bring change for his people...*my* people... through non-violent protest based on his Christian faith.

A Baptist minister, he got involved in the cause early in his career. Perhaps his shining moment in the spotlight came when he gave his now-famous "I Have a Dream" speech from the steps of the Lincoln Memorial during the March on Washington in 1963. More than 250,000 attended the event on the National Mall, making it the largest rally ever held in the nation's capitol.

Dr. King was awarded the Nobel Peace Prize in October of 1964 for his role in leading the fight against racial inequality through nonviolence. Later, he participated in a number of other rallies that gained national attention, leading the march from Selma to Montgomery.

In 1968, Dr. King was developing plans for another large-scale event in Washington, D.C., which he called the "Poor People's Campaign." But he was assassinated on April 4 in Memphis, Tennessee, and never saw this work come to pass. (After his death, the Southern Christian Leadership Conference, which he had helped found, carried on with the plans.)

Immediately upon the announcement of Dr. King's death, a wave of shock swept over the nation and the world. Not all of the responses that followed were positive. There were riots in several U.S. Cities—the exact opposite of what Dr. King had stood for throughout his 39 years of life.

I spent a lot of time processing the tragic events in Memphis. I reflected on a day not long before that when I was sitting in my office at my house and I got a call from my agent who said he had heard from the Kennedys—Ethel Kennedy, to be exact.

Apparently, Bobby Mitchell, who used to play for the Cleveland Browns, had told Ethel about me. I was invited to come to Washington, DC, for a fundraiser that would help send kids from the inner city into the country for the summer.

Their goal was to recruit their supporters from a star-studded list of "who's who" celebrities, and I somehow happened to be one of those guys. I had never looked at myself as a celebrity, but it was very intriguing to be included among all of these famous people.

Initially, I said I wouldn't go because I didn't want to fly. I would have taken the subway, a bus or a train, or driven a car to get there. I really had no confidence in airplanes.

But as I talked to my agent, he said, "Well, you know the Kennedy's are very important people."

"Yeah, I know," I responded.

I remembered watching President John F. Kennedy when he called officials in Alabama to speak to Martin Luther King, Jr., who had been jailed.

I also remembered how I felt during the tragedy of President John Kennedy's assassination and how the family all held together. I saw little John-John doing the salute as the casket rolled by. Yet I never saw one of them cry. They seemed to be standing so strong.

"Yes," I said again. "I know who the Kennedys are."

My mind instantly flashed back to that day on the practice field at the Rams camp when our coach came out and blew the whistle. We all assembled, and, of course, we thought that he was going to put us through some drills.

"The President's been shot," he tersely announced.

It was like lightning struck us. We were all stunned. Each person had his own thoughts.

Out of nowhere, one my teammates—a man I thought was a caring "Brother"—said, "They got another one; they got another honky."

Now, this was a guy who always had something to say. Something was always funny to him. He apparently saw humor in everything. Even tragedy.

I remembered another day sometime before this when we arrived at practice and he said to me, "Sam Cooke got wasted last night."

I asked, "What do you mean, he got wasted?"

"He got killed, man."

I said, "Get outta here." I couldn't believe it.

The night before, Lou Rawls, Sam Cooke, and I were planning to go together and see OC Smith singing at a club. But when I got to Lou Rawls' house, he said that Sam was not going to make it that night.

The next morning, I found out from my teammate that Sam really had been killed.

I had that thought in my mind when the Coach announced that President Kennedy had been assassinated.

When my teammate made his ignorant remark, I looked at him and thought, *He's crazy. This guy is crazy.*

I really didn't know how to respond to the violent death of our president, so I simply went down on the end of the field and I cried. I cried because this man was one of the most popular presidents we had ever had. He had inspired his fellow countrymen to get involved in compassion and sacrifice by creating the Peace Corps. He encouraged physical fitness, and he outlined a vision that would inspire our nation to land men on the moon by 1969. But his life ended too suddenly and completely.

In reality, that fateful day in Dallas nearly stopped everything. America was shocked into an awful kind of reality and watched the events that unfolded in the days ahead on our television sets. We somehow managed to play a football game that following Sunday, but there was no life in that game whatsoever.

So, yes, I knew how famous the Kennedys were and I knew what an important family they were. Even though they were a very wealthy family, they were committed to giving back to America, through military service, through participating in the political process, and through involvement with charities.

It seemed that what they wanted from me was very simple. They wanted me to spend some time with the family and gain my support for urban kids. And I didn't want to fly. I don't know why I thought flying in an airplane was so dangerous; it is probably the safest form of transportation there is. But it makes such big news when a plane goes down. And it makes such little news when so many cars crack up all day long.

Finally, my agent said, "If you go, I'll go with you."

"Okay, if you want to go, I'll go, as long as you're on the same plane with me." Off we flew to Washington D.C. I held onto the armrests so tightly throughout the entire flight that I think I had white knuckles for the first time in my life!

If you are old enough to remember those days, you'll recall that young people were always volunteering to get involved in anything that the Kennedys were doing. Students from all of the nearby colleges and universities were looking for roles they could fulfill. The Kennedys had a young group of kids pick us up at the airport and take us to their home.

When we got there, Bobby and Ethel Kennedy were already at the door to greet us. I went up to shake their hands, and, without warning, Bobby punched me in the stomach. It was an instant icebreaker. We both laughed and I took off after him and chased him down.

I spent the entire evening with him; everywhere he went, I went. He first introduced me to Byron "Whizzer" White, who earned his place in history as both a fullback for the Detroit Lions, and as an associate justice of the U.S. Supreme Court. Over the course of the evening, I met Lauren Bacall, Peaches and Herb, Connie Stevens, and many others. Celebrity after celebrity assembled to support the Kennedy's efforts. As Bobby introduced me to all of these people, I became really excited about being invited to participate. It was a very memorable event.

The next night, we had the television program and we all did our part on it. After the program ended, I went out with Peaches and Herb and we ended up at U.S. Ambassador-at-large Averell Harriman's house until 5 o'clock in the morning, yelling, screaming, laughing, and having a great time. There was a banging on the floor above us for us to be quiet. Basically, the neighbors had to run us out.

I got to know the Kennedys, and I immediately recognized that they seemed to have such a love in them. I was moved by the ease with which I fit in with them and they with me. It became natural that I would remain in contact with them from that day forward.

Members of the family would come out to California to visit former White House Press Secretary and Senator, Pierre Salinger, and have an event at his house. I would always be invited, and they would greet me by saying something like, "We were just talking about you."

Whenever I went to Washington D.C., I would be invited to their home. Prior to one of my visits, Bobby announced that he was going to run for the presidency, and I was excited. For the first time in my life, I was compelled to be involved in a political campaign. I called Bobby and said, "If you are going to run for the presidency, I'm going to help." (The truth is I didn't know what I was saying, because at that time I was afraid to speak in public.)

As Bobby began campaigning all over the country, we continued to talk about me going on the road with him. But our plans kept getting delayed for one reason or another.

One April day, I was supposed to fly to Indianapolis to meet up with him, and I was out at the airport ready to get aboard. There was a "hush, hush" that went through the airport and everybody seemed to be running every which way. Some people were crying, some were clapping, and some were laughing.

So finally, I stopped someone who appeared to be very emotional, and I asked what the commotion was about. It was then that I got the news that Martin Luther King, Jr. had been assassinated.

I had met Reverend King on a flight once. I don't know where he was going, but I was on the airplane headed back to Los Angeles. As I recall, he got off in Chicago.

On the flight we shared, I was in the coach area and he was up front. I kept looking at him and I thought, "I know this guy." He would occasionally look back at me, so finally I got up enough nerve to walk up to him.

"I know you are Dr. King," I said, "and I just wanted to tell you that I am real proud of you. I am proud of the stand that you are taking for America."

You see, I love my country. I always have loved my country, but I also love the whole world. I believe that love is the answer for all of us, and deep, sincere, life-changing love is found in God. It is in believing and thinking and acting the way God says we ought to act.

I often refer to the scripture 2 Chronicles 7:14, which says, "If my people, who are called by my name, will humble themselves and pray and seek my face and turn from their wicked ways, then I will hear from heaven, and I will forgive their sin and will heal their land." We needed to hear those words back then, and we need to hear them now.

So there I was, waiting at the airport, and I was struck by the diversity of attitudes. I couldn't believe in my heart that people could be laughing and clapping because a man's life had been taken violently. Very shortly, I got a call at the airport advising me not to come join the campaign because Bobby was going to honor Dr. King's memory by taking some days off from his activities. And he did.

I waited. Finally, I got a call to fly to Indianapolis to meet up with Bobby, because he was going back to campaigning. I got on the plane and went directly to meet up with him and his campaign organizers.

There were always a lot of celebrities around him. They were a wonderful group of people; they were all friendly and they were all filled with fire, knowing that they had a great candidate to be the next President.

That day, we campaigned all around Indianapolis. At the end of the day, Bobby asked, "Why don't you come down to the airport and meet with Ethel?"

Of course I went, and the next thing I knew, we were boarding an airplane headed for Washington D.C. We went to his home.

Now, during that time, everyone was talking about how tired Bobby looked. His advisors and friends would say, "We can't tell him to slow down, even a little, because he gets angry if we suggest he's tired."

We got to the house, and soon everyone was sitting around and laughing. I was getting to know the other people involved in the campaign and really enjoyed it.

After a while, I looked over at Bobby and I said, "Hey man, why don't you go get some sleep, because you got a lot of work to do."

Everyone stared at me as if to say, "Oh great, now he's going to get mad..."

But I didn't care if he got mad at me, because he was a small guy, and he couldn't possibly whoop me. I said it because I thought that it was good for him to get rested. There was a lot of hard work to be done in the campaign and we were out to win an election.

He looked at me as if to say, "Okay, Rosey," and he went on up to bed. Of course, we stayed up all night long, and the next day I was so sleepy that I could hardly keep my eyes open. But we campaigned hard and long every day, and flew to a number of places before I went back to Los Angeles.

While at home in Los Angeles, I stayed riveted to the campaign. I was concerned about where Bobby was and how he was doing. I was always involved because I had truly found a guy I could support. So many people gravitated to his being. He always drew huge crowds just wanting to see him.

As a result, he was always late. No matter where we went, it was very difficult to get Bobby through a crowd.

I recall a time when we were travelling through Watts. We drove in convertible cars so people could see our candidate and feel closer to him. But there was always someone standing up with Bobby in the car so that he couldn't be pulled off. We had to keep our hand around his waist.

On the ride through Watts, I was holding onto him very tightly and he said, "Rosey, you are holding me too tight."

I replied, "Well, if I let you go, you are going to fall down."

He repeated, "You are holding me too tight!" I backed off and said, "Okay," and I let go of him. He fell and I caught him, while Ethel tried to pull me back into a standing position in the car. I never heard him complain again about being held tightly.

It was always such a beautiful experience to travel around with the Senator because people loved him. They would get very emotional if he touched their hand. Sometimes when we stopped the car, he would jump off and he would go talk to the crowd, and they would put their hands on him and just begin to cry.

I believe that when there are so many expectations of a person, that person has the ability to bring about great change in society. I was involved because this was a man I was helping to bring to the American people to help us to change our attitudes.

During this time, kids were going around calling policemen "pigs" and all kinds of other derogatory names. Police had to maintain their cool; they couldn't go off because someone was calling them a name. They couldn't jump on them and beat them up. But, in a sense, I felt sorry for the police officers because uniformed police were perceived to bring negativity to the campaigns. As a candidate, you often didn't want the police to be seen because the people would boo and call them pigs and other names.

As a result, those of us who were within his own group began to take him through the crowds. I learned how to take hands of people off of him quickly without them really feeling it. If somebody reached out for Bobby, I would slap their hand away, but not with force. I would just hit it so they would stop reaching, because sometimes he would get pulled over. I would always manage to hit them just enough so that they would realize that they couldn't hold onto him. Yet he would try to shake every hand that reached out to him. Sometimes, when we get in from an event, his hands would be black and blue from shaking so many people's hands.

Even though we had an incredible campaign going on, some of the media would occasionally mount up against Bobby. They would print stories that he was ruthless and a tyrant.

I was not concerned about the names that they were calling him because I got to know the man. I never saw the side of him that they thought they were seeing. If Bobby asked me about my mom, I would tell him all about my mom and he would truly listen. I trusted him. I trusted him to be the leader of our America, and that's why I campaigned so intensely.

Candidly, my first wife didn't like it that I was campaigning out with him. She would say, "They are just using you."

I would reply, "If they are using me to help make my country great, then they can use me."

I remember one day I was at home and the phone rang. It was Steven Smith, Bobby's brother-in-law. He said, "Rosey, Bobby needs you to go over to the Brentwood Country Club."

"What?"

"The Brentwood Country Club."

I said, "You've got to be kidding me. Man, do you know what the Brentwood Country Club is?" I paused and added, "It's a bunch of rich White people, and you want me to go over there and speak on behalf of Bobby Kennedy? Uh-uh! Nope! I can't do that."

He argued, "But you told Bobby you were going to help him."

"I did say that," I agreed.

I decided from that moment on that when I would tell somebody I was going to do something I would identify what I was going to do and not do—and not be caught off balance. I was totally off balance. I never thought I would ever to have to speak in public for this man.

Despite my reservations, I said, "Okay, but I think you guys are messing up."

I showed up at the Brentwood Country Club and I saw long lines of limousines pulling up out front as I drove up in my Cougar. I found a place to park and had someone point me in the direction of the event.

There were several actors and actresses up on the stage, and they all looked so great. Lorne Greene who starred in *Bonanza* got up and spoke first. He strutted around and he knew how to walk and he knew how to talk.

When he finished, Gene Barry got up. He was dressed to the nines. Then Shelley Winters, a wonderful dramatic actress, got up, and she said, "Oh, how I love America. I love to see old glory waving to and fro in the breeze…but…what about the children." And then she started crying. "What about the children? What's going to happen to our kids who are going through all this violence?"

She was so concerned about that, she just started to bawl. She couldn't go on anymore. The host looked around said, "Rosey, you're up next," and I said, "Oh my goodness."

I stood up, and my knees were knocking. Number one, I had never really spoken before, because usually when we were on the campaign and Bobby would say, "Rosey, get up here and say something to the people," I would just say, "My name is Rosey Grier. Glad to be here. Thank you very much. Bye-bye."

Number two, I had no idea what I was going to say. Now here I was, following Lorne Greene, Gene Barry, and Shelley Winters. And I just couldn't think. *What in the world am I standing up here for? I am a cotton pickin', peanut shakin' football player, and I'm about to tell these people about the man that I care about.* Nonetheless, I began.

"Hi, Y'all. I'm not with those people right there."

The crowd chuckled, so I continued.

"I am just a cotton pickin' peanut shaker, but if I had you on the football field right now, I could drive you all right into the dirt."

Fortunately, they started laughing. And I thought, *Okay, so far, so good.* I began to share my feelings about our country, about our leadership, what I felt about our man, Senator Kennedy.

I said, "This is America, and this is our house. We all live in this house. The question is, do we care enough about our house to make sure that the things that are wrong will be made right? Do we care enough about our house that we would treat one another as we would treat ourselves? Do we care enough about this house that we live in to try and solve its problems? You see, this cannot be done by one man. It takes all of us to try to solve this problem."

The words seemed to be flying out of my mouth, so I continued, "You have not seen what I've seen. Where people would rally just to touch him or cry just to be around him or how big the crowds were, and how eager all of them were just to hear him speak. And when he spoke, it was so quiet. They listened to what he was saying. He had the ear of the people."

These words were just pouring out and all of a sudden it was quiet in the room, and I looked around. I thought, *What are they looking at?*

I looked around and I figured somebody was doing something—maybe Warren Beatty was doing something funny.

But they were looking at me.

Here were all these famous stars, and they were all there to talk about their candidate, just as I was there to share about my candidate.

As my mouth was going, I realized something: it was not the eloquence of the speech that was being made by anyone, it was what we were saying from the heart. That was the only place these words should come from. For me, that was the only place they *could* come from because I didn't know how to talk any other way. I just shared my feelings about my country, about our future leadership.

I never criticized any other opponent; that was not my job. My job was only to tell what I felt about the man that I was supporting— Senator Kennedy. That made a huge difference in my life because from that moment on, it was not just Senator Kennedy's campaign. It was my campaign as well. I became inexorably involved, and they sent me off to make a lot more speeches.

One night I looked up and one of the Kennedy sisters was there, and I wanted to know why she came. She said, "I wanted to come and see what you have been saying about my brother." Obviously, word got back to the family that people responded to what I was saying because I was not speaking so much about his policies, but I was speaking about what I felt that my country needed.

It is the same as today. You see, I feel that my country needs to stand together. I feel that there are so many negative things that are happening in our society today and we have lost our way.

At that particular time, I felt we had lost our way and we needed a strong leader. I felt the Senator was the leader that we needed. He was that drum major Dr. King talked about. He was that man who could get us back in step.

I left the platform that night to the sound of the crowd's applause, and I couldn't believe it. For the longest time, I stood alone backstage and tried to catch my breath.

I recalled a time when we were on the airplane to another campaign stop, and Bobby was talking with a group of reporters. He invited me to come over and join them.

Now, as an athlete, when a reporter was around, I was trained to keep my mouth shut. But I had never seen this particular group of journalists before, so I didn't know who they were.

They started to ask me some questions. "Why do you think Bobby Kennedy would be good for Black Americans?"

That got me going. Suddenly, I had lost all fear of speaking… of being an advocate for my candidate. "He is a wealthy man. He doesn't need to be in politics, but yet he is out here speaking on behalf of what's good for all of America. It's his belief that we are all equals."

Before that day, I was always in a rush to sit down. I would just say, "My name is Rosey Grier, and I'm glad to be here…" This time it was all about telling these people about the man that I believed would be a great leader for us. And it was surprisingly easy.

Not long after, we were at the Ambassador Hotel in Los Angeles. I thought that Bobby had a lock on the nomination—it not the presidency. The mood was one of celebration, as we were all anticipating the win.

I went down stairs to check on what was going on, and people were just partying and having a great time. Then I went back upstairs, and asked Bobby if he had anything to say that night.

When Bobby said, "Yes," I was excited because I knew the people would be eager to hear anything he had to say. But first, he had to go do a media interview.

Generally, whenever I was travelling with Bobby, I made sure to stay in plain sight so he could always have eyes on me, and I would always have eyes on him. I wanted to make sure he knew that I was looking out for him always.

I will forever reflect on that dark day. I wasn't even supposed to be at the hotel, and yet I was standing by the door when Bobby came up the elevator. As he walked past me someone said, "Come on Rosey, come on Rosey."

Up in his room, his team began to make some projections on the final result of the primary vote taken that day. When he stood up go meet with the media, he didn't have to even say anything to me. I just got up to go, too.

He walked down one side of the room and I walked down the other side, so that he could look over and see me there.

On the way to the elevator, I said, "Man, I hope you got something to say tonight, because you got the people excited and really ready to hear you and your message."

He flashed me a reassuring smile and said simply, "Yeah, Rosey, I got something to say..."

"Great." I felt happy, because he really did always have something inspiring to say. He was a great speaker; he had great thoughts, and when he was before a crowd, my chest always stuck out with pride.

When we got to the elevator to go down to the platform, we had so many people trying to get on board that I decided to wait for the next one. Everyone else jammed into the elevator because they all wanted to be with the winner.

Bobby reacted immediately. "No, hold it, hold it...Rosey, you've got to get on the elevator." So I squeezed myself in, and we went down.

While we were descending, as I was standing next to Bobby and I popped him in the stomach. "Pow!" He looked at me, and I laughed and said, "We got this one." He said, "Yeah, we got this one, now we have to go to Chicago, and heaven knows if we get that." I said, "We will. Just watch! We will!"

When we got to the kitchen area, there was a rush of people walking with Bobby, and he began to shake hands with the waiters, chefs, and the rest of the kitchen staff. He was greeting, and I was walking behind him with Ethel, but making sure she was close by him.

We entered the main room, and it was obvious that the people were so elated and having such a great time. What a joy it was to see all of these people so excited about a man who was seemingly going to win California and many of the other states—which gave him an excellent chance to be the Democratic party's candidate for president of the United States of America. Even to this day I often think "What if...?"

Bobby went on stage to make his statements, and he began thanking all the people that helped make this victory possible. He mentioned Rafer Johnson, my friend and former Olympic Gold Medalist, and then he followed that with, "If anyone doesn't support the Kennedy campaign, Rosey Grier is going to come take care of you."

Then he added, "But in a nice way, because that's the kind of people we are."

After his victory speech, Bobby was supposed to come off the stage and come back to me, and we were going to move down the right side of the room to leave.

But as he was coming towards me, the maitre 'd came out of the kitchen and told Bobby it would be quicker to go back the way we came. I was trying to prevent the group from taking that route. However, I had been charged with the care of 6-month pregnant Ethel Kennedy, so I could not leave her side.

Bobby was impetuous in a way, so he jumped off the back of the stage with Paul Schrade from United Auto Workers. Bill Berry, who was supposed to be with Bobby, was helping me escort Ethel off the stage, and then he took off. I was trying to move quickly with Ethel to catch up, when a photographer came by with a long lens, and almost hit Ethel. I blocked the photographer, but I didn't block him hard—and I know how to block hard—yet Ethel was not hurt.

All of a sudden, shots rang out. People started screaming and everyone hit the floor. I covered Ethel, but I decided to follow the sound of the screaming, because I always try to get where the action is.

When I rounded the corner, I saw people struggling with a man with a gun. George Plimpton was clearly grabbing at a handgun.

As a football player, I learned that if you take a man's legs, he can't go anywhere. So I lifted this man with the gun—Sirhan Sirhan—onto a table and I locked his legs up.

George was still struggling to get the gun, but the gun was pointed right at George's head. I instinctively put my thumb under the hammer of the gun so it couldn't fire. I was holding onto Sirhan's hand, George had the gun hand, and Rafer Johnson was up on the table trying to question Sirhan. George continued to try to take the gun out of Sirhan's grip, but couldn't get it loose.

In that instant, my mind flashed back to my childhood and the first time I ever saw my dad drunk. I came home and I could smell whiskey on him, and he brandished a gun. As he waved the gun at me and my sister, Alice, I knew I had to do everything possible to take it away from him.

She was struggling desperately, and dad pointed the gun directly at her face. I ripped that gun out of my dad's hand, I put it in my pocket, and I went out and destroyed it later.

Now, years later, here was George Plimpton with the gun pointed at his face. I finally wrenched the gun from Sirhan, found the pin and I ripped it out and held it. I shoved the gun in my pocket.

All of the other people who were at the wrong place—because we were supposed to go out as originally planned—were rushing in, only to discover that the man they were protecting, the man they loved, the beloved man they were campaigning for, had been shot down.

When they saw the person who did it being held, they went off. The guy who was standing next to me was trying to twist his legs off, and I kicked him.

I was drawn into a fight with all of the people who were swinging at Sirhan trying to get him. I was not going to let them hurt Sirhan, because had they killed him, some of us would have been in deep trouble. It didn't take them long to realize that I was not going along with their actions, so they stopped.

Not much time had passed before an emergency team came and took Bobby away. The police came and arrested Sirhan Sirhan.

I was sitting on the floor trying to recover from the shock of it all when I heard a voice asking me, "Rosey, do you have the gun?"

I said, "Yeah."

The voice said, "Give it to me."

It was the voice of Rafer Johnson.

I have no idea why I gave it to him. I had no idea why I wouldn't give it to him. I had no idea if Rafer was working with him, but I gave them the gun and I was finished. I was finished.

I went back up to the suite and everybody was all over me. They said that Bobby was going to be okay—that he had been shot in the side.

But I had seen blood when I first looked at him. I saw blood coming from his right ear. Now I didn't see anything that had obviously been hit by a bullet, but I saw blood on his ear.

Yet I'm thinking, *Maybe he wasn't hit too bad if people are optimistic.*

I remember a lady trying to take care of me, but I decided that I was going to get up and go home.

When I got home, my wife, who had said that the Kennedys were just using me, said, "Ethel Kennedy called. She wants you to come to the hospital."

So I got back in my car, and when I showed up, someone ushered me into the room where Ethel was laying on the bed beside the Senator. When I walked in the door, she turned over and she looked over at me as if to say, "Thank you for coming back," and I nodded to say, "Of course, I'm back" and so she turned back over and continued ministering to her husband.

I stood there for a while, not really knowing what to do, not knowing how to pray, for that matter. Had I known then what I know today, I would have been praying. But I decided to go back downstairs. I was standing, but it felt as if I was floating.

Joan Braden came up to me and whispered, "Rosey, I don't think the Senator is going to make it."

"What?"

She said it again. "I don't think the Senator is going to make it. I think his brain was shattered."

My heart dropped. It was the most awful feeling of my life. The man who had a chance to be president and to lead us…the man I had grown to love and admire…someone who stirred the spirit of this great country in the hearts and minds of all ages, races, and religions, wasn't going to live.

Yet, to me, she didn't seem to be all that sure. So I waited and I hoped. I waited a while longer, and then I saw Ethel and Jackie—whom I had never met—walking toward me. She was smiling in an uneasy way as if to say, "I can't feel grief."

Ethel put her arms around me. Jackie hugged me, too, and Ethel said, "My hero."

I thought, *The hero is upstairs fighting for his life.*

I didn't feel like a hero. I felt like we had made a mistake.

An hour and a half later, Frank Mankiewicz announced to the world, "Senator Kennedy is no longer alive."

Hearing those dreaded words, I felt as though thunder and lightning were going through my body. I realized that we had somehow messed up. We had missed Sirhan.

The reason I say we messed up is because we have a responsibility as people with belief and faith in God. If we do our jobs and share the love of God with people and ask people to love one another and forgive each other, then the nation would change.

Look at our nation today. We are in a jam. Why? Because many men and women of God have gone off seeking their own joy, and they have forgotten that we are here because God wants us to work for his kingdom. We weren't put here for ourselves; we were put here to glorify Him.

After Bobby passed, it was as if the world, in a sense, came to an end for me. It was the very first time I had become involved in a political campaign, and I could not believe that we weren't going to have the opportunity to elect this man to be our leader as the President of the United States. So I cried a lot.

A few days later, Rafer called me and asked me to meet him at a well-known chicken and waffle house, Roscoe's, on Pico and La Brea. At this meeting, he said to me, "Rosey, we are two of the most well-known Blacks in the world today, and I don't think we should talk about the assassination." I thought, *Well, that's okay, because every time I talked about the assassination I would just break down and cry.*

But after all these years, these events are so heavy on my heart that I simply had to share the details with you. Maybe there's a lesson there for all of us.

Rosey's Rose-Colored Gem

Because good men and women oppose evil and stand for truth, they will always be opposed by those who support evil ideas and causes. This has been true throughout recorded history. But when the battle is fought right before your eyes, and evil is victorious—even if only for a season—the pain is very real and extremely profound.

Chapter Eight

My Amazing Friend, Jackie

"I think my mother... made it clear that you have to live life by your own terms and you have to not worry about what other people think and you have to have the courage to do the unexpected."

—Caroline Kennedy

After Bobby's murder, I spent a lot of time with the entire Kennedy family. It was their hearts that drew me in. They were—and are—a very close-knit family filled with mutual admiration for, and devotion to, one another. They reminded me of my own family, only with money, fame, power, and prestige. At that time in my life, those things were all important to me. It took me time and experience to learn to replace the temporal with the eternal.

When I first met Jacqueline Lee Bouvier Kennedy Onassis, she was simply known as "Jackie" Kennedy, former First Lady, bereaved widow of President John F. Kennedy...and now the bereaved sister-in-law of Ethel Kennedy, widow of my dear friend, Robert F. Kennedy.

Jackie—I would soon learn—knew how to live every day of her life to the fullest, despite her many life-changing encounters with tragedy. Bobby's assassination was one more heartbreak on her list.

My heart broke with her when I saw the plane carrying Bobby's body take off from LAX, headed for New York.

Over the next few weeks, several people, including me, tried to shift the campaign momentum that we had been building, so that we could encourage Teddy Kennedy to run. We tried to get Mayor Daley of Chicago to throw his support behind the sole remaining Kennedy brother, but he didn't go for it. Lyndon Johnson's Vice President, former Senator Hubert Humphrey, finally emerged from the 1968 Democratic convention in Chicago as the party's choice to head the ticket—accompanied by Senator Edmund S. Muskie of Maine.

With my wounds...and the nation's...still very fresh and painful, I was very pleased that Rafer and I were invited to the Kennedy compound in Hyannis Port. It was a comfort to me that the family wasn't holding us responsible for the horrible event that had transpired in Los Angeles.

On a particularly beautiful fall day, we were out on the Kennedy lawn playing touch football. There was a little boy who kept running around in and out of my legs.

I turned to Rafer and I asked, "Who is this little guy running around here—the kid I am trying hard not to step on?"

Rafer laughed, "That's John-John."

"Really? That's John-John? Wow! Where is his mother?"

Rafer pointed and said, "Over there." I looked over and saw Jackie.

After we finished playing football, I walked over to Jackie and I said, "Jackie?"

"Yes?"

I said, "I am Rosey…" and before I could finish she said, "I know who you are. You were at the hospital with Ethel."

"Yes, I was. And now I am going to be here for a whole week. I don't have a partner, so now you're it!"

"Me?"

"Yes, you!"

"What do I have to do?"

"Let's go in the house and talk about it."

We went inside the house and Jackie Kennedy and I began to devise a plan on how we were going to challenge all the secret service men. We wrote notes to all of them, challenging them in tennis, running, shot put, and any other games we could think of.

Jackie got really excited, jumped to her feet, and said, "I'll be the captain of our team!"

"Whoooaaa, just a minute! You can't just jump up and elect yourself to be the team captain," I protested. "Suppose I want to be captain?"

She countered with, "You can't just elect yourself to be captain, either."

Finally we decided we would serve as Co-Captains. From that day forward, we always used the term " Co-Captain" as our secret signal to each other.

We spent the whole week challenging the secret service to our games. We won some, we lost some. But win or lose, we all had a great time.

I would often drive her car for her. One day we were driving Caroline to visit some of her girlfriends, and we spotted an ice cream parlor on the side of the road. We decided to pull over, and as we were standing on the sidewalk in front of the store enjoying our ice cream, a woman walked up to Jackie and began to speak.

"Mrs. Kennedy, we have something in common..."

Jackie said, "Oh yeah, what is that?"

The woman responded, "My daughter died the same day your husband was killed."

I almost fell over. Jackie did not know what to say. I realized that it's funny how sometimes people don't know what to say in certain situations. So I hurried Jackie along, because sometimes when you don't know what to say, it's better not to say anything at all.

We hung out together all week. One day, I pulled up to the house in her car, and she was already out front.

"Come quick, come quick!" she said.

I dashed into the house, and Jackie had her sister on the phone and handed it to me.

Her sister said, "Rosey, what are you all doing up there with my sister?"

I responded, "Aw, we are tearing this place apart, because no one else around here knows how to have fun, and we know how to have fun!"

Very simply, that's how our relationship began, and we became very close friends. As time had passed, I would be at home and we would spend hours on the telephone, talking and laughing, and I would play her the latest Ray Charles records.

Every time I would go to New York, I would take John-John around with me to the television stations. The Secret Service would follow him, but always in the background. They would never come near us. Jackie didn't like the secret service to be hanging around too close.

One week she called me and wanted me to come to New York, to attend a father and son dinner with John-John.

I jumped on a plane, of course.

At the dinner, John-John and I won a contest and we were awarded a silver dollar. As we were driving home, I looked over at John Jr., and said, "You know, half that silver dollar is mine." Then I added, "You get to keep it, but whenever I call you for it, you owe me 50 cents."

By the time all this was happening, my wife and I had long been divorced, and I had remarried. Of course, I told my new wife, Margie, all about my relationship with the Kennedy family, and about my friendship with my " Co-Captain." I was always talking to Margie about Jackie, and I was excited to tell Jackie all about Margie. They wanted to meet each other.

My goal, naturally, was for them to become good friends. Margie and I were invited to Hyannis Port to have dinner with Ethel Kennedy and her family. Jackie also came to the dinner. Margie and Jackie got to meet for the first time, and they had a chance to talk for a little while. I never knew what they said to each other, but Margie had lots to say about meeting Jackie.

Some time later, I told Jackie, "I want you to come down to California, because we're going to have a party." She replied, "I don't know Rosey..." and I left it at that.

After Bobby was killed, Ethel started an Annual RFK Tennis Tournament. I was all set to attend one of them in New York. That particular year, Dolly Parton was to be the guest of honor. However, something came up and she had to cancel at the last minute. And with that, we were left without a celebrity to honor that year at the event.

After thinking about it, I suggested that we invite Jackie.

Ethel protested, "Oh...Jackie won't come. She'll be too busy."

I urged her on with, "Well, did you ask her?"

Ethel came back quickly with, "She won't come, she never comes."

So I called Jackie and explained that Dolly Parton had backed out of the RFK Tournament and we needed her to come fill in as our superstar.

Jackie responded, "Oh... I can't come."

"Jackie, it's about time you come off widow's wharf, attend the party, and support your sister-in-law."

She thought for a minute. "Do you think Ethel would invite me?"

"Sure she would."

That night we were having dinner at Ethel's house and a man named George Stevens stood up and said, "Jackie, why don't you join us at the RFK Tennis tournament this year?"

And she said, "No...." You should have seen them all look at me. When Jackie left, Ethel said, "I thought you said she would come."

I said, "Ethel, I told you she would come if YOU asked her. Have you asked her yet?"

"Well no, but I told George to ask her."

"She's not going to come for George. You have to ask her, because she will come for you."

A few days passed, and I saw Ethel. She began hugging me, and she was obviously very happy. She had done as I suggested, and the next honoree at the RFK Tennis Tournament was going to be Jackie Kennedy.

I used to tell Jackie everything about everybody, so she knew the dirt on everyone. It was really fun...not that I would EVER gossip!

I was up in Hyannis Port for a week when Jackie called me in the middle of my stay and said she had to leave the very next day.

"What do you mean, you are leaving tomorrow?" I asked.

"There is a Naval Ship being dedicated to John, and I have to be there."

"Well, why didn't you tell me sooner?"

"I'm telling you now. I'm sorry, I have to go."

I accepted the fact that she had to go; however, I was sad about it. Everybody could see I was visibly affected, and the Kennedys kind of teased me. In fact, the Kennedy women always sort of poked fun at our relationship. One time, I went to a record store and bought Jackie the new Ray Charles album. When I showed up with the album, the other highly competitive Kennedy women said, "Rosey, you are always buying gifts for the rich one—The First Lady. You're always treating the First Lady nice. What about us?"

And to that I would simply reply, "Jackie is my friend. We are great friends."

Thursday came, and I expected only to hear that Jackie had left. That morning, my phone rang. It was Jackie. She said she decided to stay at the family compound an extra day, and she wanted to hang out with me the whole day. We had a great time.

Early the next morning, I was awakened by the CIA knocking at my door. They informed me that Mrs. Kennedy was waiting for me to pick her up and accompany her to the airport. I did just that. In fact, I was allowed to drive right onto the tarmac and directly up to the plane. She got out, gave me a hug, and got on the plane. I sat and watched as the plane roared down the runway and took off.

Just then, I noticed some CIA agents also on the tarmac watching the plane take off through their binoculars. I walked over to them, and said, "Hey, what are you guys doing here?"

They informed me, "We are always here. We are everywhere. It is our responsibility to know where she is at all times. In the event the plane has an issue, or makes an emergency landing, we have to be there. We have eyes on the plane for the entire flight."

Wow, I thought.

Shortly after that, Astronaut John Glenn was running for the Senate to represent Ohio. John called the Kennedys and asked for their support and endorsement in his campaign. They refused him and he was very hurt.

When I heard that, and I decided to call Ethel and see what happened. "Did John Glenn ask you guys for your support, and you turned him down? He was a great friend of Bobby's…"

She said, "Well, yes, but we can't support everyone that was a friend of Bobby."

I responded, "Do you know one time John went way out on a limb for Bobby, and he almost lost his job over it?"

Ethel reasoned, "Rosey, I know you don't understand, but we just can't do it."

"You are right… I don't understand. I love you guys, but I am headed to Ohio to support John Glenn."

Off I went to Ohio for the final week of the campaign. John was running against Howard Metzenbaum, and he had fallen behind in the polls. John's team became worried, as it seemed the tides were turning in favor of Howard.

I went to my hotel room to call Jackie. I told her everything, as usual. I told her that John Glenn had asked the family for their support and they had turned him down.

She said, "Aw, Rosey, that doesn't seem fair."

"No it's not fair, but that's the way it is. To make matters worse," I explained, "there was a leak out of Teddy's office that the Kennedys turned him down, which also has John annoyed with Teddy."

Jackie began, "Well, does John Glenn need some money to help out with the campaign?"

I cut her off. "Nah, they are not short on money..."

Then she suggested, "Well, if you send someone to my house, I could record something for John."

Surprised, I said, "You would do that?"

"Sure I would, but I'm not sure what I'd say."

So, over the phone, we started to write out what she would say. After an hour, she said, "This does not sound personal enough."

"Hmmm. Why am I helping you write something to say? I'm a football player, and you are the writer. You write, and I will get the people to your house to record."

Everything went as planned, and we got a recording of Jackie Kennedy's endorsement of John Glenn, unbeknownst to John.

The next day we took the recording to a major radio station and let it play over the airwaves. Within hours, the recording made nationwide news. Jackie's picture was in all the newspapers endorsing John Glenn for Senate. Within days, John took over the polls. And within a week, he won.

I called Jackie on the phone, and we yelled and screamed about the victory. After a few minutes of this, we took control of our emotions, and she said to me, "You won't believe what happened..."

"What's that?"

"The family called me on the phone and questioned me as to why I endorsed John Glenn."

"What did you tell them?" I was expecting that she told them what a great candidate he was, and how he was the right guy for the job.

Instead, she simply answered, "Rosey asked me to."

That's the level of trust we had in each other. It was a life lesson that taught me what a beautiful thing trust is.

Jackie was blessed with an impetuous side, too.

I was at Jackie's apartment in New York for Halloween. We were on the 15th floor, on her outdoor patio, drinking coffee and discussing what we should do for "Trick or Treat." Without warning, she jumped up and grabbed my coffee cup. She poured my coffee over the edge of the balcony where—despite her intentionally bad aim—a few drops accidentally hit a man standing below. Most of the coffee landed on the sidewalk. She ran into her apartment screaming and laughing as if she had committed some great crime—coffee on a New York sidewalk. I ran after her.

"I can see it now," she laughed. "The police are on their way. The headline in tomorrow's *New York Times* is 'Jackie Kennedy and Rosey Grier Arrested for Dumping Coffee on a Sidewalk!'"

"Waaaait a minute," I protested. "First, I didn't do anything. You dumped my cup. Second, why do you think your name always goes first? How do you know the headlines wouldn't read 'Rosey Grier and Jackie Kennedy Arrested'?"

We spent the next hour arguing that tiny little point, giggling like little kids. The fact is, when we were together we were just like big kids. We did some crazy things. I always hoped that Margie wasn't jealous, or that she ever thought there was something more to our relationship than friendship.

One day we were walking through Central Park and we saw a group of young guys playing basketball.

I said to Jackie, "Hey, do you wanna play some basketball?"

"We can't play basketball. They aren't going to let us play."

"Trust me. They will let us play. So are you coming or not?"

So I walked onto the court and stopped the basketball game.

"Hey fellas, do you think my friend and I can join your game?"

They looked at me, threw me the basketball, and then they noticed that "my friend" was Jackie Kennedy.

The next thing you know, I am standing all by myself on the court, while all the players were surrounding Jackie, mesmerized by her presence.

As we were walking away, a woman came up to us and asked Jackie to sign an autograph. Jackie stiffly signed her name, handed whatever it was back to the woman, and we kept moving.

When we were a safe distance from everyone, Jackie observed, "I don't understand it. It seems like every time people come up to us, we sign autographs, it always seems like you're getting to have much more fun than I am with the people around."

I had the answer! "Do you want to know what the problem is? You're stuffy." I laughed and continued, "You're Ms. Hotsy Totsy, snooty; you're 'The First Lady.' You have to keep up that elevated image, so you don't know how to relax and just be Jackie. You have to let the name go and be who you are."

She smiled as if to say, "I think I'll try that." Sure enough, in many instances, she did. And she succeeded.

On one visit to Hyannis Port, I said to her, "I want you to come to California."

"I can't go to California."

"Well, you're going to come to California, because I just elected you to the Board of Directors of my non-profit. So you are going to be there."

The non-profit I was referring to was Giant Step, Inc. Giant Step is an organization we put together to help disenfranchised youth who have turned to gangs and crime. We negotiated peace talks among rival gangs and created a job-training program to help them turn their lives around. After a little more prodding, Jackie agreed to come.

I decided the perfect plan would be to have a big party to raise funds for Giant Step at the famous Dorothy Chandler Pavilion. I knew that had a big job ahead of me. The Pavilion is a huge venue that could accommodate thousands of people, but it cost a lot of money to rent it for an event.

The funny part of this is that I didn't have the money to fund such an event. I walked into the Dorothy Chandler Pavilion management office and announced, "I would like to rent your place."

They asked how much money I had. I pulled a penny out of my pocket and said, "That's what I got."

They tried to hide their shock. "A penny?"

"Yeah, what I'm trying to do with my organization is to solve a problem. And if we don't solve this problem where it is now, it's going to end up at your house."

Whenever I explain that gang violence isn't just an inner city problem, and that if not dealt with, the problem will spill into the suburbs, the suburbs are usually quick to help me in my cause.

My oldest sister's son—my nephew Robert Blackwell—had come to the meeting with me. He spoke up, "If my uncle really want to do this, I will put up $25,000.00."

I turned and looked at him in surprise and asked, "Where did you get that kind of money?" Robert replied, "I've been buying and selling real estate."

I gasped for a minute...then started breathing normally.

Needless to say, we got the Pavilion for the event.

But now we needed the kinds of entertainers who could fill the pavilion!

The gang kids I worked with told me about a performer named Ben Vereen. They said, "He'll be a big star someday." I was able to connect with him, and he agreed. (I was so pleased that he actually *did* become a great star!)

I was calling everywhere, trying to get people to commit and perform for the event—to donate their time.

One day I was doing a television show, and Ray Charles was there, practicing the piano. I went over and sat down on the bench beside him. I told him my story, and Ray agreed to perform. I was on a roll!

Marlo Thomas returned my call a few days later and said, "I heard you've been looking for me, and whatever you need, you've got it." She agreed to co-host the event.

A few weeks later, I was in Hyannis Port visiting the Kennedy Compound, and I asked Jackie if she would be the "guest of honor" at my event. She reluctantly replied, "Yes."

I had been campaigning with President Carter, and he won the election. Don King called me up and asked me if I could do him a favor.

I replied, "So what do you need?"

He asked me if I could get Aretha Franklin in to sing at the Presidential Inauguration.

I said that I would try.

I immediately called Peter Duchen's manager, a man I had met at Jackie's house. I asked him if he had any minority entertainers at the Inauguration and he said they did not.

I asked, "How would you like to have one of the greatest minority entertainers of all time—Aretha Franklin?"

Peter loved it.

I told him, "I will have someone call you."

Then I called Don King back. Of course, I asked him about Aretha Franklin performing at the Pavilion. Naturally, Aretha put on a great performance at President Carter's Inauguration. But then, she came to the event in California and performed for us. In the process, she also met her future husband!

Other entertainers who helped us were the great Henry Mancini, Jackie Vernon, and Booker T. and the M.G.'s.

The next thing I knew, Aretha Franklin and President Carter both agreed to be Honorary Vice-Chairmen of the Board.

The week of the event, Jackie went all over Los Angeles with me. Not just the "nice areas," either. Yes, we were in the Country Clubs watching golf swings, but we were also in South Central, slamming dominoes. We raised money for the foundation. But as usual, we had fun—our own special way.

Not long after the very successful event for our organization, I had to visit New York, and as usual, I alerted my Co-Captain that I would be arriving in town. I asked Jackie if she could meet me on 74th St. and 5th at 3:15 p.m.—not 3:30, not 3:45, but 3:15 p.m. It seemed that, with Jackie, it helped to be very specific.

So I stood on the designated corner in New York, and sure enough, at 3:15 p.m. Jackie walked up.

"You're here! That's good. Now what do you want to do?"

She suggested a movie.

I agreed. "Sure, a movie is great."

I looked at the Limousine she pulled up in, and I expected that she was going get back in it.

Instead, she said, "C'mon, Rosey! Are we going to the movies or not?" I kept looking at her limo.

"We're going to catch a cab. This is New York."

Okay, I thought. We hailed a cab and jumped in the back. As we headed to the movie theater, the cab driver said, "Hey Rosey! How you doin'?"

Then, all of sudden, he practically swerved into oncoming traffic. He realized that Jackie Kennedy was in his cab!

We arrived at the theater and we decided to see *Yellow Submarine*, starring The Beatles.

We jumped out of the cab, and, at first, there was a big commotion—people yelling, "Hey Rosey, how you doing?" (You must remember that before I played for the Rams, I was on five world championship teams with the New York Giants. So I guess you could say I'm a New York guy, too.)

All of a sudden it got very quiet. People were noticing that Jackie was with me.

It's funny, because when people saw me, everyone would get loud and raunchy. When they saw Jackie, they would get quiet. In awe. Almost reverent.

When the movie ended, we went to the restaurant next door. After we were seated at the table, Jackie decided she wanted a cigarette. But they didn't sell cigarettes at the restaurant. She really wanted one, though.

So, I told her, "FINE. I will go back to the movies, and get you a pack of cigarettes." (Can you believe they used to sell them at movie theaters?) Anyway, I told the Maitre 'd that I was leaving, but I also told him that he needed to watch Jackie, to make sure everything went well for her.

I went. I came back.

She was fine. Nobody had bothered her. She smoked her cigarette and we ate dinner.

We were feeling good. Maybe people hadn't noticed her, and it would be a nice, uneventful evening.

Oh, how wrong we were!

We walked out of the restaurant and flashbulbs instantly blinded us. People were yelling and cheering. There was spontaneous media frenzy.

We started moving. They started moving. We began to run. They ran. We ran as fast as we could when I noticed a bus. We decided to jump on the bus to escape the media. I blocked the door so they couldn't get in, and I urged the driver to pull off. We were laughing uproariously watching the cameramen trying to run alongside to capture a few last photos. They couldn't keep up.

It was always like that with Jackie. We enjoyed our friendship a little "on the edge."

The next few days while I was in New York, I would always leave word at the desk: "If Co-Captain calls, here's how you reach me." I tried to call her a few times, but got no response.

As I was standing at the airport ready to head back to Los Angeles, a man came up to me and said, "Hey Rosey, I just saw Senator Kennedy."

At first I was steaming mad, because I thought he was trying to provoke me about Bobby. But as I continued to move along, I noticed a small area of commotion. Sure enough, there was Senator Ted Kennedy.

When he saw me, he quickly greeted me with, "Rosey, what are you doing out here?"

"I'm on my way home to LA."

"Jackie is looking for you. You better call her."

So I called her from the nearest phone booth. (Can you believe there was a time when cell phones didn't exist?)

"Where are you?" she asked.

"I'm at the airport, about to head to LA."

"Why?"

I snapped at her. "I called you for a few days. I got no answer. So I'm on the way home."

"No... you can't leave yet, you have to get back into town."

"I'm out here already. You didn't call me. So, I'm out!"

She pleaded, "There's something I have to discuss with you before you go. You have to get another flight. So come here, and I'll have the Secret Service get you back to the airport quick and easy."

I folded. I went back into New York City to meet Jackie.

We met at her apartment.

"There's something I have to do, but I can't tell you what it is."

I couldn't believe it. "WHAT? You called me all the way back into the city to tell me there's something you can't tell me?"

"I just can't tell you."

Then she laughed, pulled out a beautiful men's gold necklace, and placed it around my neck.

"You're a great Co-Captain, Rosey."

And with that—with few more words—the Secret Service came, and got me back to the airport in time for the next flight to Los Angeles.

A few weeks later, I was in Durango, Mexico, filming a movie. One day before the shoot, I picked up a newspaper and saw Jackie's picture. I didn't know how to read Spanish, but sure enough, there was her picture.

I decided I'd better call her. The person who answered asked, "Are you looking for Mrs. Kennedy?"

"Yes."

"She's not here. She went to Greece."

"Greece?"

"Yes, Greece. She's getting married!"

I thought to myself, *Aw, Woman! How can you get married and not tell me?*

I was so hurt that she felt she couldn't tell me that she was getting married.

I wrote her a long letter and sent it.

About two weeks later, I received a letter back from her. She wrote that she needed someone to take care of her—to be there for her. She said that there would always be a place for me in her life—that we could always be able to find a quiet corner. Wherever she was, there would always be room for her Co-Captain.

Whenever I would be in New York, I would give Jackie a call and she would invite me to stop by for a while. I never really had the opportunity to get to know Aristotle Onassis, but I did get to spend a little time with his daughter, Christina. She was very pleasant.

I was invited to travel to Greece and spend time with them. I immediately responded that I was not flying all the way over there, but I would build a raft and launch it in the Pacific Ocean. Her reply was to float the raft out about two miles, and she would have me picked up. She also sent a photo of John jumping off the yacht into the ocean, as well as a travel bag to use to pack my belongings. It had the name of the yacht on it, of course. That was part of our humor that we shared throughout the years.

As time went on, we corresponded less. Whenever I wanted to get a message to her, I would call her spokeswoman.

One day I got word that Jackie was sick. I tried to reach her to get permission to come see her. I got no reply.

Then I got a call from media sources telling me that the doctors were on deathwatch for Jackie. They wanted to know where I was and where would I be when she passed, so they could get comments from me. I was in Cincinnati at the time. I was very hurt just thinking that I was losing a great friend. And I did.

After receiving the news, I went back home to LA, because I knew that I would not be invited to the funeral. I was excruciatingly sad.

I got home and I was watching the big media storm over Jackie's death and the phone rang. It was John Kennedy, Jr's office. They were inviting me to the funeral and were paying my expenses to come. I said, "Yes," with tears of both gladness and sadness filling my eyes. John Jr. had reached out to his mom's Co-Captain.

At the service, as John walked passed me, I touched him. We talked later and John said that he felt happy to see me there. We became good friends. I reminded him that he still owed me 50 cents.

Rosey's Rose-Colored Gem

What you THINK you see is not always what you get! The rich and famous can be fun, fabulous, footloose, and funny! Jackie Kennedy was an interesting and refreshing lesson in that truth! She was full of unexpected surprises! Like so many friendships in life, my friendship with her was worth nurturing, protecting, and enjoying!

Chapter Nine

Decisions Are Sometimes Costly

"It's amazing when strangers become friends,

but it's so sad when friends become strangers."

—Unknown

I was certain that Senator Ted Kennedy was not going to run for president in 1980. He said he was not planning on it. I asked him to please let me know and include me in the discussion if he changed his mind and reconsidered. I always wanted to talk to the candidates before deciding if I would support them. But as far as I knew at the time, Senator Kennedy was not running.

President Carter was running for a second term. I had supported him in the first term, but he was not doing well in the opinion polls. Home mortgage rates were at an all-time high, and 44 Americans were being held hostage in Iran.

I tried to call Senator Kennedy's office several times and talk with him or one of his main staff, but I was unable to reach them. So, I called Ethel Kennedy and told her that I was not able to reach Senator Kennedy. She was very nice and said, "He does not have time to talk to everybody." I said, "Thank you. I will talk to you later."

Bill Milliken, one of the Founders of Community in Schools and a friend of President Carter's, had invited me to the White House to spend a weekend and get to know the President Carter. I initially responded, "No." I called Jackie and told her. She said it was a great honor to be invited to the White House, so I changed my mind and accepted the invitation.

I had my son, Lil' Ro, with me at the time. He was only about seven years old, so I was unsure if I could have him running around the White House with me. I decided to let him spend the weekend with the Kennedy family in Virginia. I dropped him off on Friday afternoon and headed for the White House.

I called the Kennedys on Saturday morning to speak to Lil' Ro. The first thing he said was, "Dad, you have to come get me! These kids here are too rough."

So I went back to Virginia to pick up Lil' Ro, and as we were driving up to the White House, he leaned out the window and said, "Dad, is this our new house?" I told him that the White House belonged to the American people.

We arrived late, so I tucked my son into bed right away. Despite being in unfamiliar and somewhat daunting surroundings, Lil' Ro. drifted off to sleep fairly quickly.

Before I went to bed, I spoke to a Secret Service agent about talking to President Carter. He told me that the President was making phone calls, but would stop to talk with me. When I walked in the room, he was sitting there in jeans and a tee shirt, barefoot. He asked me if I had eaten and I said "No," so we went down to the kitchen.

Someone had left ham hocks boiling on the stove, and it was smoking up the kitchen. I said, "Mr. President, why don't you leave and I will take care of this." But he didn't leave, and he took care of it. (I am imagining the Secret Service seeing the smoke, coming in the kitchen and seeing this tall black man standing by the smoke. Too bad for me!) I kind of chuckled at my thoughts.

Everything worked out. We ended up eating a sandwich. We talked for a while, and I asked President Carter, "How do you know that your orders are being followed?" His reply was, "That is why you need to get good people. The buck stops with me."

I later went to bed and got a great night's sleep. Early in the morning, I woke up and Lil' Ro was not in his bed...not even in the room.

My first thought was, *I hope he's not getting himself in trouble.* After all, I surmised, at his age he was probably not really aware of whose house he was visiting. "Leader of the free world" didn't mean much to him at that time in his life.

Of, course, I immediately panicked. I threw on some clothes and darted down the hallway, asking anyone I ran into if they had seen a little boy wandering around.

Finally, I ended up in the kitchen, and there was Lil' Ro, sitting with the First Family, having breakfast, chatting with the Carters' daughter, Amy, and having himself a grand old time!

After that visit, I spent more time with President Carter, and we discussed the many pressing issues of the day. I felt that he was truly interested in my perspectives, and wasn't simply patronizing me to gain my support.

From then on, when I would go to DC, Betty Curry, President Carter's assistant, would always make sure we had dinner together, or at least had some time to talk. I felt that I had made a new friend!

Now we all know that President Carter struggled greatly when it came to a number of issues. One was that he was not part of the "Washington Elite." But in person, he was—and is—a warm, personable man with a big heart. He is also a very intelligent man.

On one of my visits to the White House, he asked me,"Do you think I have been a good President?"

I said, "Yes."

"So I can count on you?"

I replied, "Yes."

As a result of time spent with him, it was easy for me to decide to throw my support behind him...especially because Senator Kennedy still hadn't indicated interest in competing for the nomination.

Before I left Washington, I called Senator Kennedy's office but was only able to speak to a secretary—not a close staff member. I decided I would not leave the message with her.

The President was so encouraged by my support that he announced it to the media before I got the opportunity to inform the Kennedys of my decision—and my very clear reasons for that decision. President Carter's premature statement to the press was the beginning of the end of my long relationship with the Kennedys.

Later, Senator Kennedy decided to run for the Presidency, in late 1979. But I was not going back on my word to President Carter.

Time passed and I was at the Democratic National Convention, sitting with Max Cleland, who was the Administrator of Veteran Affairs. The Kennedy girls came up to me and said, "Why did you desert our uncle? You don't love us." Before they walked away, I told them, "I didn't desert him, and I still love you."

That night I went back to my hotel really hurting. I awakened in the very early morning, and God showed me that I had idolized the Kennedy's for 12 years. I tried to love them and take away some of their pain. At that moment I was "set free."

President Carter was able to rally enough support behind him—partly due to the Iran Hostage situation—that he was able to defeat Senator Kennedy in 24 out of 34 presidential primaries... more than a two-to-one margin.

I took to the road on behalf of President Carter, but my support had little, if any, impact on the results of the election of 1980. The President was defeated by a former movie star and California governor, Ronald Reagan, 50.8% to 41%. (John Anderson also ran as an Independent that year, and got about 8% of the vote).

After the election, I agonized for weeks, because President Carter had lost. Then I started paying attention to the newly elected President, Ronald Reagan, the 40th president of the United States. I believe in supporting the president the people want to lead them, demonstrated by their votes. My eyes were no longer just on the athletic field, but on the community around me.

Rosey's Rose-Colored Gem

One of the most difficult challenges in life is to rebuild a bridge that you—or someone else—have burned. It may require patience, time, and a huge measure of forgiveness, but it *can* be done! As you will see.

Chapter Ten

From Football To Tv To The Big Screen

"What makes it all worthwhile is we just play for the sheer enjoyment of entertaining people and...make our families and the team we played on and the people watching, proud of what we did."

—Bobby Hull

Acting—on the stage, in film, or on television—is not for everyone.

First of all, for the most part, the entire process is incredibly boring. It's often been described as "hurry up and wait," or, "about as exciting as watching paint dry."

Everything about it is extremely slow moving. There's makeup (and that can take hours sometimes), and lighting (setting it up and getting it right is an art—and a chore), and rehearsals (which never seem to end), and re-takes (which can number in the dozens). As with many other endeavors in life, the real excitement is in the end result. It's in watching it all come together on the screen—or on the stage.

But, other than the slow-moving parts, I loved everything about acting! I not only loved the end result, but I also loved the teamwork! The dramatic arts are not just about the "drama" portrayed by the actors.

It's true beauty is when all the arts and crafts come together, focused on a single, perfect result. Everyone has a job to do: the writers, the casting agents, the set and prop designers, the director, the actors, the stunt performers, the lighting technicians, the cinematographers, the editors, the sound mixers, and the music composers and performers.

When I was acting, I was just one little cog on a huge wheel. But I loved being that cog!

I appeared on dozens of shows beginning in 1964. I considered every show—and every TV star I met—to be a great honor. After all, I was just a rather large football player who was mostly used to knocking opposing players down.

Now, all of sudden, I was on the set with Robert Vaughn and David McCallum on *THE MAN FROM U.N.C.L.E.* (No, it's not about their Uncle!) The stars played secret agents who worked for a fictitious secret international espionage and law-enforcement agency named U.N.C.L.E.—which supposedly stood for the

"United Network Command for Law and Enforcement." It was a creative and entertaining show, and I was proud to be a part of it!

Some time later, I was in a Hollywood studio with Barbara Eden, playing a role on *I DREAM OF JEANNIE*. For most actors of the time, that was a "dream come true." She was—and is—a beautiful, vivacious, engaging, and talented woman!

In 1969, I was contracted to appear as a regular cast member on the TV series, *DANIEL BOONE*, starring Fess Parker. I have a great appreciation for American history, and while this show was not entirely historically accurate, I felt honored to be a part of bringing this slice of pre-Revolutionary War history to TV viewers.

I was a regular on *MAKE ROOM FOR GRANDDADDY*. In one of my appearances on *THE WHITE SHADOW*, I got to wear my Number 76 jersey from my playing days with the Los Angeles Rams. I was on *CHiPs*, and two episodes of *KOJACK* as well as on *THE LOVE BOAT*, *MOVING ON*, and *QUINCY, M.E.* I was even on game shows! One of my more recent television "appearances" was when I did the voice for a character on *THE SIMPSONS* in 1999. The episode was called "Sunday, Cruddy Sunday."

Ah, the memories! My "career" in television was a rewarding experience!

On the other hand, the movies I appeared in were not quite as "high profile" as my TV appearances. They were mostly low budget films: *THE THING WITH TWO HEADS* and *THE GLOVE* among them. (And no, *THE GLOVE* had no connection whatsoever to O.J. Simpson—a topic I'll be discussing in an upcoming chapter.)

Despite how slow-moving and boring it is to be on a movie or TV set and wait for the next thing to happen, I loved it. I loved the people! The experience drew me out and gave me more courage to speak in public.

Up to that time, my life had been football. Then it was acting mixed with politics. In every setting, I loved the people with whom I was privileged to work. I loved the players and coaches, both at the college level and the pro level—and even in high school. I loved the people who wanted to serve in government to make our nation—and our world—better for all of us.

But sometimes, people in the entertainment industry take a bad rap. The media are always chasing them down, hoping to catch them doing something wrong. In the course of my acting career, I learned that these people have feelings, as we all do. They are not so thick-skinned that they are immune to criticism—especially when it is mean-spirited.

If they happen to make money doing what they love, they are always confronted by a long line of people who want to take their money away from them. If they achieve fame, there are always jealous people who want to see their fame disappear and their popularity vanish.

Then there are the entertainers who act like they are "owed" something. They don't realize that, in the eyes of God, we are really all the same.

No career choice that puts someone in the public eye is an easy one, whether it's sports, entertainment, or politics. In politics, especially, death threats are numerous, and sometimes carried off.

My joys—in football, entertainment, and politics—came from active participation, from seeing the outcome, from meeting and getting to know wonderful people, and from bringing smiles to peoples' faces. That made it all worthwhile for me!

Rosey's Rose-Colored Gem

No matter what career path you choose in life, you can use it to bring smiles to the faces of other people. I've noticed that lots of people who work at Southwest Airlines know this. It's part of their corporate culture to be friendly and fun...almost like family...a *funny* family!

Chapter Eleven

Kids Say The Darndest Things

"The most interesting information comes from children,

for they tell all they know and then stop."

—Mark Twain

Many of my older readers will likely remember Art Linkletter. For my younger readers, Art was a TV host back in the days of black and white television. (If you can imagine such a thing!) One of the shows he hosted was *KIDS SAY THE DARNDEST THINGS*. (Bill Cosby did a similar show years later.)

The basic idea was that a lot of great wisdom—and humor—flows out of the mouths of kids.

Little did I know that there would be a pivotal time in my life when wisdom would flow out of Lil' Ro's mouth, when my son would say the darndest things.

When I was 40 years old, I married a lady named Margie Hanson. We got married for all the wrong reasons. Neither one of us knew about real love. For a time, we were friends and we were happy. But we had no foundation about the truth of what a marriage was, so it was not long before we were living like we were before we got married. She did not seem to have her own friends, and I knew nothing about her past. That was one of her secrets. I only knew that she had been divorced.

But—and I say this as lovingly and respectfully as I can—she was also incredibly expensive. She honestly believed that because I was an ex-NFL player and knew the Kennedy family and was pursuing a career in the "glamorous" entertainment business, that I had a bottomless bank account...that the checks could just fly out of the checkbook without any thought whatsoever.

Not only that, but she was a big tipper. She thought of herself as a "compassionate tipper," whereas I was an "ordinary tipper." So while I would give a skycap $20 for handling our two bags, Margie would tip $50 or $100 for the same service. "I'm sure he has a family and needs it," she would say in her defense.

Basically, Margie spent money as if I were an oil baron. Or a steel magnate. Or a Kennedy.

I thought to myself, *If this keeps up, I'm gonna die a poor old Black man living on the streets of L.A. and picking my food out of garbage cans.*

So I made what I thought was the only reasonable decision available to me at the time. In 1978, I divorced her and I moved out of our home, so that she and Lil' Ro could stay there.

Lil' Ro was 4½ at the time. I supported them, took care of the payments, and Margie was able to stay at home and not have to support herself. I was also paying alimony to my first wife.

At the time of my separation and divorce, I lived in the Oakwood Apartments in Burbank. I thought I was going to have such a good time because I was "free" and single again. But there was an aching and emptiness in my heart. Nothing seemed to satisfy that aching.

Margie and I shared custody of our son, Lil' Ro, and I loved every minute I spent with him.

When he stayed for the weekend with me, Lil' Ro and I used to talk a lot about God. He was especially intrigued by the idea of Eternal Life, although neither of us knew much of anything about it.

"Dad, do you think there is any way people can live forever?" he asked one day.

"I don't know, son."

Lil' Ro thought for a moment, and then he had an idea!

"If we move to Alaska and live in an igloo, the cold weather would make our bodies slow down, and we could live longer!"

I had no idea where he got these kinds of ideas. But he continued…

"Do you think God would want us to do that?" he asked.

His questions…and ideas…would keep me going.

One day, I thought, *Is my life just all about paying two alimony payments?* Then I thought, *Black people do not commit suicide.* So I just went on.

I amused Lil' Ro by giving him a little red wagon that he would ride down the gentle hill near us. But he had bigger plans.

He looked at a mountain that was near us, and he wanted to go on a hike.

One weekend, his mom was visiting us. I didn't especially want to spend time with her, so I decided to take Lil' Ro on the hike up the mountain. On the climb, we had to go through lots of overgrown bushes. Lil' Ro got scratched by the branches, and didn't like that at all. So he decided to go back down the mountain and spend time with mom. Remember, at the time, he was only about 5.

I called after him. "Lil' Ro, when we start off toward a destination, we don't turn back."

His mom was watching him this entire time, but he didn't know that. Yet, she knew the struggle he was going through.

Lil' Ro turned around, and using a stick he had found along the way, he pushed the branches aside to make his way through the bushes. Along the way, he fell into a hole, and he begged me to pull him out. You may not agree with my response, but I believed that he had all the tools and resources he needed to get out on his own. I hollered, "Use the stick to get out!" And he did!

That afternoon, we did what we set out to do. We went all the way up the hill!

In the meantime, his mom left, but Lil' Ro and I were so proud of ourselves! He couldn't wait to tell her!

Some time later, a friend of mine named Carl Johnson came over to see me. Carl was once a coal miner in West Virginia, but he came out west to help me reach out to kids in the inner city—what we now call the "Urban Area."

He knocked and knocked and knocked. I didn't want to let him in, but I finally gave in and opened the door.

His first words were, "Rosey, God sent me to see you." That really annoyed me, but there was nothing I could really do about it.

Then he looked around the room and saw the Bible that he had sent me from Israel. He asked if I read it. I said "No," and I asked him to leave. I was depressed. I didn't really want to talk about the Bible, because it didn't seem to have any answers for me. So Carl left.

The next day, I had to fly off to an event half way across the country. I didn't want to go...I didn't even want to see the sunlight. But I had committed, so I knew I had to get on that airplane.

Early in the flight, an attractive flight attendant asked me, "You're Rosey Grier, aren't you?" I said, "Yes, I am." Then she started to invade my space—something I didn't really expect. She started talking about a man she knew who talked about the Bible on television. She said, "He's a Black man...and a great teacher. I think you'd like him."

I said "Thank you." But I didn't really mean it. I wasn't looking for "Bible talk."

Later on in the flight, she approached me again. She said her name was Ann Luddick, and she asked me for my phone number.

I thought to myself, *Well, she IS cute,* so I gave her my number.

The following Sunday morning, my phone rang.

"Hi, Rosey, my name is Ken Luddick. My wife is Ann. You met her on a flight a couple days ago. She's a flight attendant."

"Oh, yeah," I said. "I remember." I knew about the cute part, but not the married part. Oh, well.

He continued. "Rosey, watch Channel 11 at 8:30 tonight. I think you'll like it."

He added "God bless you," and then he hung up.

With no idea what I was about to watch on Channel 11, I turned on my TV.

The first thing I saw was a choir singing a song. I had no idea what the name of the song was, but the lyrics talked about "evidence." The song raised a question: If I were to be tried in court for being a Christian, would there be enough evidence to convict me?"

Well, I was sure there wouldn't be, but it was a really "hip" song, so I continued to watch the program.

Then this "Brother" walked on stage. I had no idea who he was. His name: Reverend Frederick K. C. Price. He was the founder and pastor of a huge church in Los Angeles. And he was unlike anyone I had ever seen or heard before. Despite that, I was captivated.

In the middle of this program, I decided to call my ex-wife, Margie. Lil' Ro answered the phone, and I told him about what I was watching. He turned on his TV, watched Fred Price's telecast, and we agreed to talk later.

Every other weekend, we watched this man on TV together.

"Dad, let's go to church," Lil' Ro suggested after one night's telecast.

"I don't want to go to church."

"Dad, I've never been to church."

I wasn't just saying that. I really *didn't* want to go. I thought back to when my dad used to make me go to church as a kid. *Well, it didn't kill me,* I thought to myself.

"Okay, Lil' Ro, we'll go sometime," I agreed.

"How about tomorrow?" he pressed.

We got up very early Sunday morning, and the entire valley was totally socked in with a thick fog. We got in the car, but I couldn't even see across the street.

"I'm sorry, Lil' Ro. Do you see how foggy it is? I can't drive in this. It's dangerous."

"Dad," he admonished me, "when we start out for someplace, we don't turn back."

Smart kid. He figured out how to turn my own words against me.

We inched our way to church through the fog.

When we got there, I was surprised to see a line of people stretching around the entire building. I couldn't believe it. *We'll never get in,* I thought.

However, our "hosts" had seemingly thought of everything. They had an express line for visitors. We got right in.

I was immediately struck by what I would describe as an "electricity" in the church...and in the people who were there. The closest thing to this I had ever seen was in a championship football game, or at a rally with Bobby Kennedy. But this was a *church*!

I noticed that they all had Bibles. *Man, we've come to the weirdest place!*

Then the choir sang a couple songs…with a lot of energy.

When they finished, the man we had seen on television—Rev. Frederick K. C. Price—stood up and talked for a couple minutes about tithes and offerings. *Uh, oh, here we go,* I thought.

The response of the audience really surprised me. Instead of balking at the idea of giving, they were applauding and waving envelopes containing their checks and cash in the air. I would have to describe their attitude toward giving as enthusiastic—even "cheerful." I decided to put a few bucks in an envelope. I didn't want Lil' Ro to think his old man was cheap.

Then Fred Price began to talk from his heart.

"I have a question for you. Do you know why you have to be born again? It's because of Adam and Eve. They sinned, so every man or woman born after them has been born into their sin. That's why Jesus had to come down from heaven to earth, to die in our place. It is his free gift to us…to give us a 'second birth.'

"There are actually three deaths. There is physical death, when our bodies die. There is spiritual death, when we turn away from

Christ, and there is eternal death…when our rejection of him means that we will be separated from God forever."

I had been so depressed for so long that I could barely explain why I started to feel a certain relief—a release—coming over me inside.

At the end of his lesson, Reverend Price issued something I now know is called an "Invitation." It was his call to invite us to believe.

He said something like, "I know that there are people here whose lives are a wreck."

I looked around the room. *How did he know I was here*, I wondered.

He continued. "Your answer is a relationship with Jesus. With all eyes closed, and all heads bowed, right where you are, I am asking you to simply raise your hand above you if you would like to be introduced to Jesus Christ and his answers for your life."

I timidly raised my hand a little bit, then I raised it higher.

Reverend Price then said, "If you have raised you hand, that means God is speaking to you, so please stand up right now."

I stood, and suddenly a lifelong dam of stubbornness broke inside me, and I started crying. I hadn't been to church in at least twenty years, and here I was, standing in front of a huge crowd, crying like a baby. I looked down at the little boy standing next to me, and Lil' Ro was standing beside me, his hand raised…and he was crying, too.

Those of us who had responded were led to a counseling room. The counselor asked me why Lil' Ro had come. I answered, "He came for me."

"No dad," little Rosey interjected. "I came because I need Jesus."

It was a new beginning for a dad and his son.

A couple Saturday nights later, Lil' Ro was again spending time at my place. Out of nowhere, he asked, "Dad, can we invite Mom to church?"

To be honest, I didn't want to take her anywhere for any reason. But Lil' Ro begged: "Dad, Mom needs Jesus, too!"

So I finally gave in. "Okay, we'll do that sometime."

He took that as a definite "yes" and immediately called his mom. "Dad wants to talk to you."

I reluctantly took the phone and asked Margie if she'd like to join us for church the next day.

"I'd love to," was her response.

So, of course, we took her to church.

At the end of the service, Margie raised her hand and stood up—just as Lil' Ro and I had a few short weeks earlier.

The three of us got involved in a training class so that we could learn more about our newfound faith in Jesus. I came to understand what Jesus meant when he said, "Let the little children come to me, because they are of the kingdom of heaven." The teachings of the Bible truly are something that children can understand!

After several weeks of study, all three of us decided to be baptized together. I was still dealing with depression, so a friend told me I should move back in the home with Margie and Lil' Ro. I also discovered that my attitude toward my ex-wife was changing.

One Sunday, Pastor Price was preaching about "Shacking Up," which was what Margie and I were doing. He said that a person couldn't be a Christian and live that lifestyle. So I decided that Margie and I should get remarried. We were remarried by Judge Kenyon in our home.

We told Lil' Ro when he got home from school that afternoon. The first words out of his mouth were, "Why didn't you invite me?"

Margie and I spent the next 31 years together. There were many challenges and ups and downs. Our foundation was not stable for our marriage, because we both had brought secrets and lies into the relationship. This is something that I will talk about later.

One of the "downs" was when she came to me one morning and said, "I need your prayers, because I am going to have to have an operation." She had a miscarriage after we got together, and Lil' Ro and I were both so disappointed. Lil' Ro was hoping for a new baby brother or sister.

Six years flew by from the time Margie and I got separated and divorced to the time we got remarried. But if it weren't for the fact that kids say the darndest things, we might never have gotten back together.

"Dad, Mom needs Jesus, too!"

Thanks, Lil' Ro!

Rosey's Rose-Colored Gem

It really doesn't matter where wisdom comes from. All that matters is that you learn the lesson you need…when you need it. My children have provided lots of wisdom to me—at the exact perfect moments!

Chapter Twelve

The One Thing I Thought Would Never Happen

"Sometimes I can't help but feel the first amendment is being turned on its head. Because ask yourselves: Can it really be true that the first amendment can permit Nazis and Ku Klux Klansmen to march on public property, advocate the extermination of people of the Jewish faith and the subjugation of Blacks, while the same amendment forbids our children from saying a prayer in school?"

—Ronald Reagan (Presidential Radio Address,

February 25, 1984)

I was born a Democrat. I was named after a Democrat— President Franklin Delano Roosevelt. I was raised a Democrat. I supported Democratic candidates and voted Democrat for much of my life.

Then something unexpected happened. After my candidate of choice, Jimmy Carter, lost the 1980 presidential election, I started to take a closer look at our new president, Ronald Reagan.

I saw how the new president's positions stood in contrast to the popular positions of the day. Reagan was a former Democrat himself. Why did he change parties? Why did he "rethink" his politics?

I wanted to know. And I wanted to know how his personal beliefs could possibly align with mine. I was a Democrat, after all!

Now, I fully realize that no ideology is perfect. No political party gets it 100% right. No leader in the political arena is perfect.

But as I began to look at the issues—both those that unite us and those that divide us—I began to sort through what is important to me, and what is of lesser significance.

Some examples: I really don't believe that any of us—no matter what party—want people to starve, or to die of some terrible disease, or be deprived of a meaningful education. That seems to me to be common ground. The debate is more about how to achieve those noble ends.

I also don't believe that race should be in a bottomless pit of inequality or lack of opportunity. I'm sure that many of you knew that I was going to say something like that. But you need to know that I have never regarded or used color as either an advantage or as a disadvantage. The reason I got paid "adult wages" for picking cotton when I was five-years-old is because I worked hard and proved myself and I earned it. I never said, "Hey, I'm just a little boy…I want my share…I deserve it 'cuz I'm just a little Black kid. So, gimme, gimme, gimme."

That would have been wrong thinking then, and I think it's wrong thinking today.

So, I hope we agree on the basics: Life, Liberty, Opportunity, Education, and the Pursuit of Happiness.

During those days, Ronald Reagan highlighted two other issues that have become increasingly important to me over time. These are the issues that contributed to a great divide in America in Reagan's era, and they are still divisive today.

Prayer in Schools…and in America in general;

and,

Protecting the Unborn.

I remember the time when most Americans—Democrat and Republican—agreed that we were "One Nation, Under God, With Liberty and Justice for All." Yes, I realize that the words "Under God" were only added to the Pledge of Allegiance in 1954, although "In God We Trust" first appeared on our nation's coins in 1864.

But for most of my life, I have believed that we lived in a nation where God played a major role. Even in the decades of slavery, Blacks realized that maybe, just maybe, our common faith could draw us together. After all, the great Negro Spirituals of years long gone by had become reasons for hope and faith.

I remember that day I first heard the revered epic jazz singer, Ethel Waters, sing the great song, "His Eye Is On the Sparrow." It was the lyric right after that: "And I know He's watching me" that convinced me that she knew what she was talking about. I didn't fully realize the depth of that statement initially, but I somehow connected with it.

Ronald Reagan helped me understand that God had His eye on us—and that not everyone understood that fact. Nor did they understand why that's important—why it really mattered. As much as I disdained it, we were…our nation was…divided. We were not the "one Nation, under God" that had been our dream and goal. We were not the nation that the Reverend Dr. Martin Luther King, Jr., had envisioned. We were, in fact, becoming "One Nation…or Many Nations…*without* God."

Nothing in my recent memory demonstrated the great spiritual divide between the two main political parties—Democrat and Republican—than the proceedings at the 2012 Democratic National Convention.

The people who drafted the party's platform left "God" out of it entirely.

Did you watch this unfold on television? I did. The leaders on the stage took three votes—all vocally. I'm convinced that the "Nay" votes easily outweighed the "Yay" votes in every instance. The majority of Democrats wanted to keep the words "God" and "Faith" from being a part of their official political platform.

This was all a huge departure from the party of Presidents Roosevelt, Truman, JFK, LBJ, and Carter.

Three votes, some say rigged results. Many of the more liberal delegates threw a fit when the resolution to include "God" in the official platform finally passed—rigged or not. Many Muslims were especially agitated by the outcome.

I could basically see this trend in the Democratic Party falling into place many years ago. What Ronald Reagan did for me is convince me that America could either be FOR God or AGAINST God. I have chosen to be FOR God. 100%.

So after Governor Reagan defeated President Carter, I wrote him a letter. I said, "Mr. President, I am here for you if you ever need me in any way…for any reason." That's the way I have always done things. If someone I support loses, I always write to the winner. My goal is to always be a "Uniter," rather than a Divider. This is MY country!

Now, I had met President Reagan when he was the Governor of California. But when he came back from a tour of Vietnam with

Bob Hope, I refused to go meet with him because he had cut off some of the funding for mental illness. When I get behind a cause, I simply don't compromise. To me, mental health is a worthy cause.

Yet, much to my surprise, President Reagan responded to my letter. After that, we communicated quite a lot, and I spent time with him in the White House, making my case for various social issues—all as a new-born Republican.

Early in President Reagan's first term, I was in Washington, D.C., and I heard that he was trying to get voluntary prayer back in schools. All the people I had worked for in the past had voted against voluntary prayer in schools.

Some good friends from the world of sports and I were invited to the White House. The meeting was set up by Bill Keyes, a key assistant in the White House. While we were there, Meadowlark Lemmon, Demond Wilson and I prayed for President Reagan and laid hands on him. The President's response cemented my relationship with my newfound political party.

As the 1984 elections approached, I was in Minnesota for an event when I got a message from the President. He was at his ranch and he wanted me to call him back.

"Roosevelt, I understand there is a possibility you'd like to help me in the coming election. Is that true?"

I had already given this considerable thought. "Yes, Sir, I'd be happy to do that."

"May I announce that to the press?" he asked.

I thought back on how President Carter's premature announcement to the media had impacted my relationship with the Kennedys.

I responded, "No sir, I messed up before when I let President Carter announce my support, and the Kennedy's and the press jumped all over me. I was known as a Kennedy man. They felt that I had become a traitor."

The President understood completely. Shortly thereafter, I went to a press conference where I made my own announcement. There were some "Kennedy People" there, but that did not deter me.

"I like where the President stands. I think he's a fine President, and he has done a good job. He supports prayer in schools, and he sees prayer as a vital part of our way of life. Our nation was founded on prayer."

Helen Thomas, who was one of the most famous and respected reporters in the history of White House press conferences, asked, "How can you be a Reagan man? Can you see what he's doing to the minorities? He has cut off so many important programs."

I said, "Ma'am, I am not a Reagan man. I am God's man. The President is not responsible for everything that happens in our world or our country. There are so many others who have to play significant roles. Sometimes, as individuals, we need to be responsible for ourselves. In the Bible, Second Chronicles 7:14 says, 'If my people, who are called by my name, will humble themselves and pray and seek my face and turn from their wicked ways, then I will hear from heaven, and I will forgive their sin and will heal their land.'"

Of course, what I didn't explain to Ms. Thomas is that there are key words and phrases in those words that we need to fulfill as our responsibility to God: "Called, Humble, Pray, Seek, and Turn." When we do that, God's promise is to "Hear, Forgive, and Heal." As a nation, we weren't doing our part. And I believed that President Reagan was calling us back to God.

My reply to Reporter Thomas was, "God will make provision for all those people you're talking about. That's not the President's job. His job is to be the president for ALL of the people...not just for some."

I said it then...and I believe it now. The President's job is to be the president of all of us.

My relationship with President Reagan evolved over the years. It turned out to be fun! President Reagan and First Lady Nancy had a playful side to them that I really learned to appreciate.

I was in Florida when I got a phone call from the White House "scheduling secretary." President Reagan wanted to know if I would like to join him to watch the Super Bowl. Super Bowl? White House? But of course!

The Washington Redskins were playing the Denver Broncos. The game was played on January 31, 1988, at Jack Murphy Stadium in San Diego, California. It was the first time that the Super Bowl was played in there.

When I got to the White House, I was in awe of the other guests. They included Henry Kissinger, Colin Powell, Vice President (and later, President) George Herbert Walker Bush and his wife, Barbara, and Billy Graham. I thought, *What in the world is going on here? I'm the only football player in this group.*

The Washington Redskins were down 10 to 0 at the end of the first quarter. It was not looking good. Out of nowhere, I exclaimed, "Okay, now we're going to see some real football."

Sure enough, Denver never scored another point. Washington went on to score 42 unanswered points—35 of them in the second quarter. They won 42-10!

I was so proud of Doug Williams. He had experienced a rough road to the Super Bowl. But he became the first Black quarterback to win the NFL Championship. He was also named MVP.

President Reagan was elated with the victory. He asked me, "How did you know that was coming?"

"I didn't, Mr. President. I just believe that America really IS the land of opportunity." To me, it's not about race. It's all about giving equally talented people an equal shot at the prize.

I had brought a Bible that I gave to Mrs. Reagan that night. "Call me Nancy," she said. She really appreciated it. What a warm and caring individual!

Billy Graham, a man I have held in the highest esteem since I first heard about him and his ministry, was also wonderfully gracious. His driver drove us back to our hotels. It was a kind and memorable gesture!

Over the years, the President invited me to several State Dinners. I shook hands and talked with numerous world leaders, including Margaret Thatcher, Great Britain's Prime Minister at the time.

I even had the opportunity to ride with the President on Air Force One...quite an honor for anyone who gets invited, but especially for a cotton-pickin' football player from Cuthbert, Georgia.

On one such flight, I was sitting at the back of the plane (no, it's not the same as sitting at the back of the bus "Down South!") and one of the President's staff came back to see me.

"Mr. Grier, the President would like you to join him for dinner. Would that be okay with you?"

How would you respond? I could either sit in the back of the plane with the press corps, or I could have dinner with "Ronnie."

Well, I said, "Yes." And I enjoyed a wonderful private dinner with the President, the First Lady, and Frank Sinatra—in my opinion, the greatest crooner who has ever lived! I asked President Reagan if I could pray before the dinner and he said, "Yes." And did I ever pray—praising God as the Spirit moved!

On another day, I was in Washington, and the President invited me to go to George H. W. Bush's house for $10,000 per plate dinner. (Thankfully, my plate was free. It was an okay dinner…but the food was NOT worth $10,000!)

As I was leaving, I wanted to talk to Vice President Bush. I fumbled for the words a bit, but I finally said, "Mr. Bush, you should be honored to be the Number Two man in the world. You were elected to take over for the President if you have to." President Reagan had already been the target of an assassin's bullet, so that was—and is—always a possibility.

I offered these words to Mr. Bush because I felt that people, and the press, were always needlessly picking on him, and I wanted to encourage him. I wanted him to be proud!

When I changed political parties, it was for two primary reasons. Two of my closely held principles. The freedom to pray anywhere and anytime—especially in schools! – and the right of the unborn to enjoy the gift of life.

You may not agree with these principles. As I said, no one gets it 100% right, 100% of the time. We all make mistakes. We all make uninformed decisions—and even informed ones that don't work out.

I believe I have made the right ones for me. I have no regrets.

Rosey's Rose-Colored Gem

Give yourself the freedom to change your mind, refine your beliefs, and grow. Just because you've always done things one way doesn't mean that there couldn't be a better way. To discover it, you simply need to be open.

Chapter Thirteen

I Discover A Real Treasure

"I want to thank Mike Milken for the wonderful work he's done, for the focus on bioscience and its promise to expand the length and quality of our lives."

—President Bill Clinton

What thoughts pop into your mind when you hear the name "Michael Milken?"

Whatever they are, I want to correct some of the myths you may have heard because few people in public life have been as widely praised and, at the same time, as indiscriminately criticized. Like John D. Rockefeller, Milken created a new business model for those who followed. But unlike Rockefeller, who concentrated on industrial power, Milken's lifelong goal was just the opposite—he sought to "democratize capital," a quest that grew out of a personal epiphany during the 1965 Watts riots in his native Los Angeles.

But who is this man, really?

Esquire magazine listed Milken among "The 75 Most Influential People of the Twenty-First Century." *Vanity Fair* said he is part of "The New Establishment." *Fortune* magazine called him "The Man Who Changed Medicine." But ask Michael what he has achieved, and he will tell you he has "created value." He sees the process of value creation—whether in medical research, finance, public health or education—as essentially the same: Apply an entrepreneurial approach that seeks out best practices and empowers people to change the world. It is never, he stresses, just about writing checks.

Michael Milken began working on Wall Street in 1969 and financed the growth of more than 3,200 companies that created millions of jobs. But he didn't fit the buttoned-down Wall Street image. So when some ambitious politicians began looking for an issue—a "political football," so to speak— in the 1980s, they latched onto the disruptive changes that were sweeping securities markets. Michael Milken was an easy scapegoat.

Company executives, whose old-fashioned, inefficient ways were being challenged, complained to the newspaper publishers who sought their advertising dollars (just as the politicians sought the newspapers' endorsements). It was a perfect storm that engulfed Mike in a linked triumvirate of angry competitors, scandal-hungry media, and politically ambitious prosecutors.

It was during this time that my family had the opportunity to meet the Milken family. The Brentwood School on Sunset Blvd. in Los Angeles is where we sent our son, Lil' Rosey to school. The Milken children also attended that school. I had no idea how much this would really cost, but, nonetheless, he was there. When I asked his mom how much tuition was, I almost fell over. It cost more than a public school teacher's salary for an entire year.

At one of the many fundraisers the Brentwood School held, the Milkens bid $11,000 for a pot of gumbo that Margie, my wife at the time, was to make for a later event. The fundraiser dinner was held at Gary and Nancy Freeman's house. Their son, Zach, was one of Lil' Rosey's schoolmates. I went, and I was sitting next to a woman I had never met. I asked her name, and she told me her name was Sandy Milken, the wife of Lowell Milken. I was impressed, because the Milkens were financial geniuses from Wall Street. I couldn't wait to meet Michael and Lowell.

When I was around Michael and Lowell at other events, I wouldn't talk. I would just listen, because I wanted to discover how to be a better businessman and learn how to serve my fellow men and women better.

As the government and press attacks on Michael grew, I called his office to see if I could schedule a meeting with him. Michael agreed, and his assistant gave me a time to be there. When I arrived, the first person I met was Michael's sister, Joni Milken. She was really friendly, and she loved athletes. I learned that her favorite NFL team was the Raiders.

I was ushered in to meet with Mike. Of course, I had my Bible with me. I showed him the Bible and said, "This has the answers to your problems. Now you are going to find out who your real friends are. I am here for you, and I am willing to do whatever I can do to help. But I guarantee you that you are going to be a 'bigger man' after you have gone through this. People are going to empathize with you because of this trouble. They will be able to understand that this kind of thing could happen to them as well."

Mike had helped arrange a loan of 900 million dollars to Reggie Lewis, a Black businessman. At that time, the major lenders were advised not to lend money to the Black CEOs of companies. Michael's life was threatened two or three times for doing that. He was also often asked why he would loan that kind of money to a Black man, and he said, "I didn't loan money to a Black man, I loaned money to a businessman." He also loaned money to other minorities to go into business.

Following his release, Mike did what any sensible man who had been away for two years would do. He went to a doctor for a complete physical. He asked for a PSA test. His doctor protested: "You're too young for that."

Mike insisted. The doctor gave in. When the results came back, Michael was informed that his PSA was seriously elevated. Further tests indicated that he had prostate cancer. The doctor told him, "You have between 12 and 18 months to live."

You might think there could be nothing worse than receiving that kind of devastating prognosis, especially after his legal challenges. But if you ask Mike what was the most difficult experience of his life, he will tell you it was his inability, despite his Herculean efforts, to save the life of his father, who died from cancer in 1979.

Mike began immediate treatment and fought this newly discovered threat with everything he had. The experience changed his life—and mine. He concluded that there was something he, in his position, could do on behalf of cancer research. He was already the co-founder of the Milken Family Foundation and the chairman of the Milken Institute. But he also became the founder of what was later called the Prostate Cancer Foundation, the world's largest philanthropic source of funding for research on the disease.

This organization was started in 1993, 20 years *after* Mike's first philanthropic gifts to support work on breast cancer, melanoma, epilepsy, and many other diseases. It became a model for dozens of other disease-specific organizations that today have joined in a multi-disease network under *FasterCures*, a center of the Milken Institute.

In a November 2004 cover article, *Fortune* magazine called him "The Man Who Changed Medicine," honoring his approach to funding and the results that he has helped achieve. *Fortune* stressed the changes he wrought, not just the checks he wrote: "No one had ever really pulled together the full picture of how—and how much—[Milken] has shaken up the medical establishment and saved lives ... Now thousands are living longer—and leaders everywhere are taking notice."

At the time, I was working in San Diego 10 days a month trying to prevent the proliferation of gangs—and also working to improve the lives of senior citizens. I was being paid $50,000 a year. The county started to lay people off, and a reporter for the newspaper wanted to know, "Why is Rosey Grier still working there, if the county is laying people off?" An article in the *LA Times* said that they were going to let me go.

As I was finishing out my contract of that year, I received three calls as a direct result of that article: one from the Rams, one from

Ralph Shapiro, and one from Richard Sandler and Lowell Milken on behalf of the Milken Family Foundation. They wanted to meet with me.

I called Margie and told her that they were going to let me go. She said, "What about the contract?" Then, I went back to the head of the county and said, "Pay me $50,000 for the rest of my contract and it will be all right." I worked for the rest of the year on the contract and then left San Diego.

I met with Richard and Lowell, and they offered me a job working with them. I decided to be up front with them. "You can't afford me," I said. I knew my budget, I knew that the cost-of-living increases continually, and I was determined that I was not going to work for a charity for free—or nearly free—no matter how important I believed that charity to be.

To my surprise, Lowell suggested that I write down my budget, and then he handed me a slip of paper. I wrote down my numbers and handed the paper back to him. To my further surprise, Lowell and Richard both looked at my numbers and smiled. Lowell said, "Rosey, you need to make more than this to take care of the taxes."

So we rewrote the budget, and I became a Board of Trustees Member for the Milken Family Foundation and a Board Member for the Prostate Cancer Foundation, formerly known as CapCure.

I currently serve as a Program Coordinator for the Milken Family Foundation.

Today, another 20 years have gone by. Mike and Lowell have created a new "home" for me...a place where I care about my "family" and where we enjoy mutual, unending support. They have also given me the freedom to pursue my interests on the outside. I would have to say that these two gentlemen truly understand how it all fits together. We help one another. That's how life works when it's working at its best!

And speaking of "fitting together" and helping one another, I worked to bring together a Board of Advisors for the Prostate Cancer Foundation. Through Senator Ted Kennedy's staff, we reached out to him to join the board. His staff basically gave me the run-around, perhaps because they'd read inaccurate stories about Mike Milken's past.

I was in Kansas on a business trip, and a woman gave me Senator Ted Kennedy's home phone number. I called him and woke him up. I said, "I am sorry that I woke you up." He responded, "I am sorry, too."

I told Senator Kennedy about the team that Mike Milken was putting together—a foundation to fight cancer. We wanted him to be on the Board of Advisors. I told him that his staff had given us the run around, so I decided to call him at home.

Senator Kennedy said, "Remember when I wanted you to help me when I was running for the Presidency, and you didn't? SO, I'm not going to help you, either." He concluded with, "I'll pray for you, and you pray for me," and hung up before I had a chance to respond.

I couldn't believe that he turned down the opportunity to be involved in the fight against cancer. After all, the reason I had supported President Carter was because Senator Kennedy had initially said he was not running—and he made no commitment to run until after I had given my support to President Carter.

And he was still angry with me?

I decided to call Mike to offer to resign from the Board of Directors, because I did not want his foundation to be involved with my decision to let the media know what had happened with Senator Kennedy. Mike told me to come home and talk to him first.

By the time I got back to the office, I had written a letter to send to the media. Michael read the letter and said, "He (Senator Ted Kennedy) is a very powerful man."

I responded, "But not more powerful than God." Mike said that we did not need the Senator. I replied," Okay, but I am going to write him a letter." And I did.

Then I told Mike that I was going to try to get all the former Presidents of the United States to be on the "Presidential Board." He smiled and said, "If you can get one, that would be good." I was *determined* and said, "I will get them all."

Within a few months, the five living U.S. Presidents were on our Presidential Board—Presidents Ford, Carter, Reagan, George Bush, Sr., and Clinton.

President Bush. Sr. was first to agree, then President Ford. I knew that President Reagan was going to be easy to get on board.

But President Carter gave me the runaround. I called his son, Chip. I said, "Remember, I lost my relationship with the Kennedys because of my relationship with your dad. I campaigned hard to get him re-elected. So when I call to speak to your dad, I want to get through to him."

Chip understood. I got through to President Carter on the next call. His honest response was, "I won't be able to do a lot of things to help, but I'd be happy to lend my name to your cause."

That was enough for me! I'd rather that people be straightforward with me, instead of making a lot of empty promises that they know they won't keep.

Every time another former president agreed to serve, I would celebrate. They all loved what Mike was trying to do for the good of humanity. They understood the complexity of his past. They simply got on board.

Today, a photograph of the five presidents standing together is displayed on the Prostate Cancer Foundation office wall at the Milken Family Foundation headquarters in Santa Monica, California.

I believe that they all knew the "real heart" of the man whose organization they had agreed to support. America really is a place where the truth about someone will eventually emerge. Milken has met with the Presidents—most recently, with President George W. Bush and President Obama. He has also met with the heads of state of the United Kingdom, Russia, Israel, Singapore, Albania, Rwanda, Iceland, and Mexico.

In 2012, President Obama invited Mike to the White House—along with Warren Buffet, Bill Gates, and other members of the Giving Pledge, an effort to help address society's most pressing problems by building public-private partnerships. The goal was to encourage the world's wealthiest individuals to give more than half of their wealth to philanthropy or charitable causes, either during their lifetime or in their wills. The world is finally recognizing who the real Mike Milken really is.

In Mike, I met a real treasure who, in his heart, wants people with life-threatening diseases to have their best chances.

I am both honored and privileged to know and work with Mike and his entire family.

Rosey's Rose-Colored Gem

Since the first ships arrived in the "new world" and we became America, the "American Dream" has inspired people everywhere. I believe in that dream—the idea that anyone can get ahead based on intelligence, hard work and triumph over adversity—not their race, religion or ethnic background standing in the way.

Chapter Fourteen

O.J.

"I'm absolutely, 100 percent, not guilty."

—O. J. Simpson

I was one of millions of Americans transfixed in front of their television sets on June 17, 1994, when we learned that a white Ford Bronco was being pursued by police on a "low-speed" chase on a Los Angeles freeway. The driver of the Bronco was Al Cowlings, a former NFL player and a close friend and former teammate of a passenger huddled down in the back seat of the vehicle.

The passenger, of course, was football great O.J. Simpson, who, police suspected, had murdered his ex-wife, Nicole Brown Simpson, and her friend, Ronald Goldman.

I watched these events unfold, live, on national TV, at the home of Keith and Katie Phillips. It was their son's graduation, and we were celebrating.

Of course, I had a high regard for O.J. as a player. When watching him smash records, I often thought, "Even my friends Lamar (Lundy), Merlin (Olsen) and Deacon (Jones)—as the starting defensive line of the Los Angeles Rams— wouldn't have been able to stop this guy. He's fast. He's smart. He's tough."

I had never met O.J. After his illustrious football career, most of it with the Buffalo Bills, he turned to acting in Hollywood movies, and became the well-known "star" of the Hertz commercials— running through airports and magically flying through the air and landing in the seats of convertibles.

But this day, he was being pursued at 35 miles per hour by at least 15 police cars and more than a few helicopters. As I watched the live coverage that day, all I could do is ask endless questions… and pray.

I remember praying, "God, I don't know anything about this whole thing. I don't know O.J., and I don't know what he has done or hasn't done, but I pray that he gets home—or wherever he is going—safely.

The chase did end at O.J.'s beautiful house, where he was taken into custody. He was imprisoned for the murders of Nicole and Ron. All of the surrounding events and accompanying drama became the "media circus" of the decade.

O.J. was a football player whom all of us—former players or not—admired and respected. But now, I simply saw a man in deep trouble.

Of course, I never played against O.J., because we were separated by a lot of years. But I was very impressed by his great achievements at USC, and later in the NFL—in Buffalo and in San Francisco.

I always hoped to meet him, and I did come close one time. I went to a fundraiser that he and Marcus Allen were attending. I got involved in a conversation with Robin Williams and, as you might guess, he was telling endless comedic stories and doing rapid-fire impressions. He's a funny guy, and, that night, he was almost unstoppable. When I got free from the conversation, I sought out O.J., but he had already left.

My son, Lil' Ro, actually met O.J. before I did. His schoolmate and friend, Hamilton Von Watts, lived next door to O.J., sharing a back fence property line, and he and O.J.'s kids often played together in the neighborhood streets. My wife used to see Nicole Simpson walking down the street in our area, and she would sometimes spot Nicole in the local Starbucks.

There was just such a hysterical fascination with this story. The media had turned it into the biggest drama on television. Never an hour went by without breaking new information on the Simpson Story.

I had so many agonizing feelings about the tragedy. I felt so many emotions thinking about the Goldmans, the Browns, and O.J. Simpson and his family.

I was watching all of the drama on television one day when Brian Weaver, a friend of mine, called me and suggested that I visit O.J. in prison.

"Why?" I asked.

"Well you are a minister, and I haven't seen any ministers around him."

I got to thinking about it. "I should go visit him because he is in serious trouble, and if he doesn't know the Lord, he needs to."

So I went down to the jail and met with the chaplain. The chaplain told me that if I produced my ordination papers and a letter from my church, I would be able to enter the facility.

Of course, I got them and went back to the jail. They hadn't called for me. No one had called for me to go down there—I just went on my own.

Upon arriving at the prison, I asked the guard to "Please tell O.J. that Rosey Grier is here to see him, but if he doesn't want to see me, it was alright because nobody had sent for me to come. I came on my own, but I would like to see him and talk to him."

I sat and waited. I sat there with a big Bible that I liked to carry with me.

After a while, the guard came back and said that O.J. would see me.

Now, I had no idea what I was going to say to the man, but I just knew that when I saw him, God would give me the right words. (Yes, I really do believe that!)

I went through the lockup, and they took me into a back room and sat me down to wait. After about half an hour, three deputies entered an adjacent room with O.J. We were separated by a glass window.

O.J. was patted down, shackled around his arms and waist. It reminded me of a mummy in chains. They chained him to the floor on his side of the partition and unchained one of his hands so that he could hold the receiver to talk with me.

I said, "Hello, O.J."

He responded, "Hello."

"I know you don't know me," I began.

He responded, "I know you."

I showed him my Bible and said, " O.J., I have watched you all of these years playing football, and I have just missed meeting you on a couple of occasions. But I think I can help you, and this is how." Again, I showed him my big Bible.

I said, "I hope you don't mind."

"I don't mind, because you want to make sure that my soul is saved."

"You got that right."

I sat there and listened to him talk for a few minutes. He bared his soul.

"Why would anybody think that I would kill my children's mother?"

I let him vent. I listened. Then I began to share the Word of God with him.

I'm not exactly sure where I started, but I made sure to tell him that God loved him. We spoke mainly about the scriptures. Of course, at that particular time, he didn't have a Bible, so I had to do all of the reading.

As I read the Bible, he had some amazing questions that he wanted to ask. It wasn't like, "Why me, Lord?" He had deeper questions.

I told him that he had been trained, that he was the only person who could go through what he was going to go through. I told him that God has prepared him well.

We spent a lot of time just talking about the Word of God, and I read scripture after scripture. I discovered through our conversations that he really is a brilliant guy. He wanted to compare himself to Job, and I didn't object in any way, because a lot of people want to compare themselves to Job—mainly because they don't truly understand the meaning of Job. He thought Job was simply a guy who had endured lots of troubles—as if he were being punished.

As far as I understand it, Job was a man who never lost his faith in God. He taught us how to hold firm to our beliefs. Even in the face of tragedy and horrendous trials for him and his family. Even when his friends advised him to give it up, he stayed faithful.

While I was there, Robert Shapiro, one of O.J.'s attorneys, came in. He thanked me for coming to visit with O.J., and he immediately asked, "Do you know exactly why you came to visit O.J.?"

"Of course, I know why I came. I see a man who is in trouble, and my purpose as a minister is to come and try to help him during these difficult times."

He responded to me in what I thought was a peculiar manner: "Remember why you came."

I thought that was a very odd thing to say to me, but after I left, I understood what he meant, because when I stepped outside there was a wall of media coming at me with cameras and microphones.

"Rosey! Rosey! Did you see O.J.?" They shouted out questions.

"Yes, I did."

"What did you talk about?

"This." I held up my Bible.

"How does he feel right now?"

"Like I'm telling you, I came to talk about the Bible. I didn't come to bring messages or thoughts or opinions. I came to bring THE Message...the Message about God and his love for all of us...for O.J."

As hard as they pressed, they couldn't get anything out of me... because there was nothing they *could* get out of me.

Every time I came to visit, the media was there. And they asked me the same questions every time. I gave them the same answer every time.

But there was one time when I came out and they were literally smothering me.

"What did you talk about today?" they all asked.

"We talked about the Bible, and about how he feels about God."

"What in the Bible did you talk about?"

Well, of course I took that as a great opening!

"We talked about why Jesus came and died on the cross for our sins…how His purpose was to give us the chance to be part of the family of God. I told him that throughout the greatest battle of any man's life, God is always there."

When I said that, the reporters all began to fade away. All of them except for one. He was a Black guy who felt very comfortable talking with me.

He said, "Rosey, I'll bet you don't see any of that in the papers tomorrow."

He was right. I was telling them about the single most important truth I know, and they didn't want to hear it—or report it. Sometimes I think that PC—Political Correctness—is a real enemy of the truth.

O.J. was ready to hear the message, but the media wasn't.

Initially, I saw O.J. two to three times a week. Part of the reason was that his family requested it.

I remember that they called me one Sunday morning, and said, "O.J. is having a tough day. Would you go see him?"

So, of course, I called the prison commander and got permission to come in at the last minute. I went through involved sign in and entry procedure. Then I sat there waiting: 30 minutes…45 minutes…an hour. Finally, I went to see the officer in charge.

"I came to see O.J., and he's not here yet. Usually it doesn't take that long."

He acted extremely annoyed, but he didn't even respond to me.

I paused for a moment, then I said, "Every time I come here, I treat you with respect…respect for your position. I expect the same from you. I expect you to be considerate of my time."

He just stared at me. So I continued.

"People who are in cells here have loved ones who are NOT in prison, and they deserve your respect. They didn't do anything wrong. This will not happen again!"

"What do you mean?" he asked.

"I mean, this is not proper…I am here to bring hope to a man. No matter what the courts eventually decide, he is human."

Finally, O.J. was escorted to the visiting area. He was really upset; really crying. "Why? Why am I in here? Why am I being treated like this? Why would people think all these things?"

I shouted at him to get his attention. "O.J.! O.J.! Hold it, man. Hold it! You are under an attack. The Devil has your mind going. He is trying to mess you up. Hold fast to the Word of God, O.J. Trust in God. He will see you through this time."

I tried to comfort him with words from Scripture. As we started talking about the Word again, the Lord moved in and calmed this man.

O.J. always understood that I wasn't there to talk about his guilt or innocence. But there were others who weren't at all convinced about that.

In the midst of all this, I had to go on a business trip. My wife called me at my hotel one night. She sounded distraught.

"What is it, Margie?

"You won't believe what happened. The papers are saying that O.J. confessed the murder of his wife and Mr. Goldman to you."

"You're not serious!"

"One of the guards came to them and said that he heard O.J. confess to you that he was guilty of killing his wife and Ron."

Again I said, "You have got to be kidding me."

"No, that's what he said. Not only that, but Judge Ito is going to go over there tomorrow and check the place out."

Naturally, the media showed film of Judge Ito going to the prison where the guard said O.J. confessed to me.

I couldn't believe what I was hearing—and I couldn't wait to get back to refute what had been said.

Shortly after my return, I was informed by O.J.'s lawyers: Johnnie Cochran, F. Lee Bailey, and Robert Shapiro. Johnnie Cochran informed me that I should sign a confidentiality agreement. It basically said, "Being a minister, there were certain privileges due me, and that I had no authority nor did I have to speak on anything that was told to me in confidentiality as a minister by another person. I did not have to express what was shared."

I agreed, of course, knowing full well that O.J. had not admitted anything to me.

Prior to the trial, I prayed with O.J.'s attorneys, asking God to specifically guide their questions to uncover the truth. God is a God of truth, and truth is what He is really interested in.

I was subpoenaed to come to court. Now, of course, that day I was not dressed for court; I guess I could have dressed better. First they asked me the question "How long have you known O.J.?" and I answered "I had never known O.J.; I met him the first time when I came to prison."

Every time they asked me any question about O.J., his lawyers would object and the Judge would say "Don't answer that." So whenever a question was asked of me, I would first look at the Judge. It was an amazing thing. As the prosecutors were pursuing O.J., I never went to the courtroom except for one time as a witness. I went again when the defense called. I prayed with the defense attorneys.

Every time I was on the witness stand, I was asked very pointed questions by the prosecutors. With every question, O.J.'s legal team shouted "OBJECTION!" almost instantly.

I looked in O.J.'s face in that courtroom. I could tell that he knew I would testify honestly, and he had nothing to fear.

When there was no objection, I would look at Judge Ito strait in the eye and answer honestly.

Somewhere in the midst of the lengthy trial, a fight—a disagreement— surfaced between F. Lee Bailey and Robert Shapiro. I got a request from O.J. asking me to talk to them.

I called F. Lee Bailey in Florida. I asked him, "Do you know why you are on this case?"

He replied, "Yes."

"Is the case about you?"

"No."

"So why are you and Robert Shapiro having problems on the case, when O.J. Simpson's life is at stake?"

"Well, Shapiro is trying to get me fired."

I said, "It is not about him, it is not about you. You guys are defending O.J. and his life is on the line and you guys are engaged in petty fights. You need to back away from all that other stuff and get on with the case; it is not about this other stuff. They need to see you guys united."

"Well, if he would back off of me, I would back off of him."

So I called up Robert Shapiro and I said the same thing to him about him and the other attorney working together as opposed to being apart. "You guys are demonstrating that you're not together—that you're not on the same team. You have a great responsibility here. You have to do better than that. For O.J.'s sake."

When the conversations ended, I had no idea if my words had been heard or not. But the next day we were in court, they showed up arm-in-arm.

I think Robert Shapiro gave way to Johnnie Cochran. They all played their part in dismantling the prosecution's accusations.

As the trial dredged on, it became the most watched trial in history. It was a real life soap opera. It was often called "The Trial of the Century."

The prosecution attorneys—Marcia Clark and Christopher Darden—brought on a variety of witnesses, and the defense team's responsibility was to refute the validity of the witnesses' testimony; and they did a good job.

There was a point in the case where the prosecution was presenting shoes prints at the scene of the crime, and they were the type of shoes that O.J. had been seen in. They used those shoes to try to pin the crime on O.J.

They produced gloves for O.J. to try on, and he could not get the gloves on his hands. They were far too small. "If it doesn't fit, you must acquit," became Johnnie Cochran's famous catch phrase.

Our nation was extremely divided throughout the trial. This tragic event had affected three families. I offered to meet with the Browns and Goldmans and pray with them and for them. I wanted them ALL to know that I understood their hurt…their pain. They informed me that they all had their own clergy. I hoped they would accept my offer, but in my heart, I knew they wouldn't. They saw me as aligned with O.J.

When the trial ended, O.J. Simpson was found "not guilty." The verdict was met with cheers, with jeers, and with downright disgust.

Shortly thereafter, the Goldman's filed a "wrongful death" lawsuit against O.J., and, in the ensuing trial, Simpson was found guilty, and the Goldmans were awarded a monetary judgment. In some ways, I think that amounted to "double jeopardy." "If you can't get him one way, get him another way."

The bottom line is that I accepted the fact that it was not my responsibility to judge O.J. Simpson, nor to judge the judicial system.

For me, it was the same with Sirhan Sirhan. There is no doubt that he assassinated Bobby Kennedy. I was there. So many others were there. Since that horrific time, some have called for Sirhan's execution. But taking another life could not restore Bobby's life.

After O.J. was acquitted, I turned down most of the requests for interviews from the media. I did not invest my time with O.J.

for media fame. I invested it for O.J.—to clearly light the pathway to God through His Son, Jesus Christ.

But I accepted some of those requests. One of them was with Gloria Allred. She had gone on TV and called him a murderer. My response to her was, "You should be ashamed of yourself; you are supposed to be a lawyer, upholding honor and justice, and here you are calling the man a name, and he has been tried by a jury of his peers and found unanimously not guilty." To me the case had been decided.

I remained in contact with O.J. after he was released from jail. Though he moved from place to place, I wanted to keep him in the Word of God. I wanted to help him build his faith.

I continued to follow O.J.'s life when he moved to Florida. I have tried to reconnect with him in Nevada, where he is serving time in prison for another unrelated crime.

The reason, of course, is that I still care deeply about his eternal soul. I want him to know peace…and life everlasting. That is what God desires for all of His children.

Despite my sincere attempts to reach out to O.J., we have not talked again.

Rosey's Rose-Colored Gem

I'm grateful that I don't have to decide who's innocent and who's guilty. I'm perfectly happy to serve God, for he knows the truthful answers to all questions.

Chapter Fifteen

People Care...Or Not

"Too often we underestimate the power of a touch, a smile, a kind word, a listening ear, an honest compliment, or the smallest act of caring, all of which have the potential to turn a life around."

—Leo Buscaglia

People who know me well know that I cry. Big tears. Lots of them. All of them real, none of them fake.

In fact, I actually recorded a song about crying many years ago. It was titled "It's All Right to Cry," and I did it for Marlo Thomas's TV special, *FREE TO BE YOU AND ME*. It was about gender stereotypes. You know...why would a big NFL defensive lineman do needlepoint? Why would a young girl play with toy trains and trucks?

Most of my tears are cried over people who are missing out on the lives that *should* be theirs. City kids lost in the pit of street gangs are especially close to my heart.

When it comes to these kids, too many people have given up hope on them. Often, a young person's journey down the dark path to destruction begins with parents who don't care. These kids may come from single-parent homes where mom works long hours to keep things together. They may come from homes where one or both parents are drug addicts or may be in prison. Sometimes it's the grandparents who do the "parenting," and they are often unable to gain and maintain control.

It breaks my heart. It makes me cry my "grown-up" tears.

You've probably read news articles or statistics about these unfortunate situations. These kids often get lured into street gangs and then get hooked on drugs. Then they get involved in crime or prostitution to support their drug habit.

When many people see kids roaming around the streets in gangs, they see a lost generation of urban thugs mired in drugs and violence...kids without hope. After all, that is what the public sees on the news.

When I look at these same kids through my Rosey-colored glasses, I see kids with a desperate need for self-esteem, for acceptance, for a feeling of worth and purpose. Every young person has those same deep-seated needs, but the kids in gangs don't have the tools or the framework to express and fulfill those needs in positive ways. They may have been raised in homes where there was little or no money, or where one or both parents were serving in prison. They may have failed in school, and fallen in with a crowd of other discouraged kids who feel hopeless. They may have had everything, but the devil is out to steal, kill, and destroy.

That's why my heart goes out to them. Every person has dreams. Every person has hopes. Every person is beautiful and special and has value. The problem is, vast numbers of those who live in "inner cities" don't recognize or accept that awesome, life-changing truth.

Worse, they don't believe that anyone outside the "hood" really cares. Corporations don't. Institutions don't. Faith-groups don't.

One Thanksgiving morning, a headline in the newspaper announced that a three-year-old girl had been killed by a "gang-shootout." Of course, she was not involved, but she was out walking with her mother, got in the line of fire, and was killed. I started crying. I thought, *Somebody has to do something about this.* Police have many challenges and obstacles in preventing those kind of tragedies, so I thought I would try to find a way to help.

I decided to go into the community, sit in the park, and observe. I saw a lot of young men moving around in the park, but I just watched. Usually if someone wanted to make contact, he or she could simply bring dominoes and ask, "Are there any domino players out here?" and get a game going.

But I simply sat there. Finally, a young man named Fred Horn recognized me, came over to me, and asked, "Why are you out here, Rosey?"

I told him that I wanted to meet some of the kids. He responded that he knew a lot of the kids. He had an organization called "Anti-Self Destruct" and he spent a lot of time talking to the kids. He focused on kids that were going the wrong way.

Fred told me that I could hang out with him and maybe even become part of the board of his organization. I suggested that I would like to hear him talk and learn what he had to say.

I went to a meeting with him, and maybe 50-60 kids were standing around Fred as he talked. What he had to say was outstanding, so I decided to join his board.

Fred Horn was very straightforward. "You young men think it is great to make a young woman pregnant, but you do not have the money to pay the hospital bill or take care of the lady and the baby. And you young ladies, you think to prove that you are a woman, you have to get pregnant. And now you look for help, because you cannot take care of the baby alone. You look to your mother, grandparents, or other relatives to help you." They just listened, they were not angry and seemed to be taking it all in. They understood honesty and truth.

I followed Fred around the communities for a year and a half. I never really tried to talk to the kids—I was just being friendly.

One day, Fred called me at the office and said that the kids would like to hear what I had to say, because I had been around them for a long time. He picked me up at the Mayor's office where I was working as a community adviser. Of course, I had already retired from pro football by this time. I had also worked for Eugene Kline, who owned the San Diego Chargers and a chain of National General Theatres.

Fred talked to me in the car on the way to meet the young men and women. He said, "When we get there, you are on your own. Don't look at me for anything." I thought to myself, *Hmmm!*

When we arrived at the Jordan Down Projects, there were at least 400 kids outside. They did not say a word as I got out of the car. They didn't say "hello" to Fred or me as we walked through the crowd to go inside the building where their leaders were. When we got inside, they started the conversation with, "You have been hanging around us for a long time. What do you want?"

I said, "I just want you all to know that I love you." I heard several "groans" from the leaders. Their response was, "We do not want any preaching!"

I told them "I am not hear to preach. I just want to let you know how I feel about you, but I do not like that you are killing one another. There is so much you could really do. I admire you for your boldness, but as opposed to the 'heroes' you should be, you are called 'gangs.' And that is a big difference."

Then I added, "And I can help you."

The spokesman's street name was "Fast Black." His real name is Michael Tobin. He asked, "Do you want to help us make some money?"

I said, "Sure! If you want to work and get a good job, we can do that."

Fast Black responded, "Who sent you?"

My reply was, "Nobody."

"Who's paying you?"

"I'm not getting paid to come and see you. I'm doing it on my own. "Do you want a job?" I asked.

"Yes," Michael Tobin said.

I avoided using their street names when I talked to them, just as I would recognize any other young man or woman by their given name. I did not want to acknowledge their street names.

I said, "Okay! I want you to stay right here. I am going to go find out about some jobs for you."

"Fred, will you take me to the mayor's office?"

He said, "Let's go."

So we arrived at the mayor's office and I said it was urgent that I speak to Mayor Bradley. He was the first Black mayor of any major city in America. I thought I just might have a chance to see him!

Mayor Bradley came out to talk to us. I told him where we had just come from and why we were now in his office. I introduced him to Fred and explained what we were trying to do. I told him that we needed his help. Mayor Bradley thought for a few minutes then said, I can give you 15 slots."

I said, "Thank you so much", and headed back to Jordan Downs.

The young people were still waiting, although they really didn't expect me to return. Back inside, I told them that I had 15 jobs waiting for them right now and I asked, "Who wants to work?"

Not one hand went up. It was totally silent!

Then Michael Tobin said, "I'll take one." He was the only one. So I said to the other guys, "How about you?" NOTHING! They figured it was a "set-up."

Michael Tobin met me in my office at 9:00 the next day, took a job, and we remained in contact for 30 years—until he died of natural causes.

I filled the other slots with one football player, three young Hispanic men, two young ladies, and other young men and women from all demographics.

They would go out into every councilman's district and find out what was going on in the communities—both good and bad. We would have meetings every day and discuss what they had found out. Then, they would go out again the next day.

That continued for some time. Then we began to report to each councilman about his district and the problems that were going on in their neighborhoods.

The councilmen determined that I had too much influence over the kids, and they did not like the reports that we were bringing back. They soon decided to take the young men and women and start a "round table," create a fund, and have them come in and report. Generally, when a fund is created for such purposes, it is not going to last. And it didn't.

We had created a voice and a support system in the community for these young people. We stopped rumors, prevented wars, and brought some peace in several situations. We also got senior citizens involved with the young people and they had "senior proms" and other events. We even shot a major pilot movie in the community with some of the kids in it. It was a three-day series called "Sophisticated Gents." Friends gave us jobs, and more youth were working and making some money.

The kids would appear on local television shows and they would get to talk. When a "call-in" would try to "bang" on them, I would stand up for the kids. I told them that these shows were to teach the community and how to make it better for everyone—not for people to call in and vent their frustrations and tell the kids how bad they were. They already knew that.

Then the money ran out, and the support from the political community ran out. So the kids returned to their old ways, and the gangs started spreading all over the country. The kid's prophecy about everyone coming in with a big show and leaving when the money runs out happened again. Except for one thing: I did NOT leave them. I was still there, and I am still there today.

Calls asking about our efforts started to come in from all over the country.

I decided to answer San Diego's call. Jesse Arnelle, the first Black president of any major university in the country, Penn State, called me. He said, "An alumnus of Penn State, Norm Hickey, would like to meet with you about working with him in San Diego to prevent the proliferation of gangs there." This became another turning point in my life. I took the job he offered for ten days a month.

I also got to meet Estean Lenyoun, who lived in San Diego. His personal goal to be the first Black billionaire. He started out working for his dad in a gas station, and bought his first car when he was twelve years old. He couldn't even drive yet. Later, he began to buy and sell property. His holdings grew to $50,000,000.

Estean started living "high," flying all over the world, and he got involved in wanting to create a major deal in Utah. Using recreational drugs became a way of life for him. Of course, the money went away quickly.

But the good thing was that he fell in love with Jesus. And his beautiful wife, Karen, stuck with him through it all. He eventually became an assistant pastor. That is when we met—thru Jim Hatcher, who was an assistant to Norm Hickey. Norm Hickey was head of the county business affairs.

I liked Estean and we started talking. I was very impressed with his business expertise. I wanted him to commit his life to work with me to change the inner cities, starting in San Diego. We both got very excited, and we are still excited and still going today. We have achieved many incredible things.

Estean approached me about the possibility of investing in—and renovating—a run-down apartment complex consisting of several buildings. He thought it was a community that we could turn around with "tough love."

I shook my head. "Estean, my brother, it can be done, but you are talking about a real challenge." My heart told me it would be worth a try. So we decided we would go to the board for approval.

We bought the buildings and we put "tough love" into action. "Wanna pull off a drug deal? You're out! Wanna turn tricks under the porch? You're out!"

This was an entire community made up of four-bedroom apartments—and 85% of the tenants were on government assistance. This complex had the reputation of being a hotbed of criminal activity, with prostitution and drug deals going down in broad daylight. There were approximately 1,500 phone calls to the police every year.

We took some of the land and built a safe, supervised playground and park for the kids. We painted. We repaired sidewalks and broken windows. We planted lots of greenery. You would not believe the "before" and "after" pictures.

We asked Maranatha Church and their pastor, Ray Bentley, to have Bible studies in the community to give it a spiritual foundation.

Estean and I had formed an organization, Impact Urban America, to oversee and accomplish all of this. We realized that meaningful employment would be of utmost importance to those living in the complex. Our organization developed an employment agency called WORKS. We thought we might be able to get 50 people from the community employed and generate a few hundred thousand dollars in the community. But the first year, we employed

1,000 people and turned over $1,000,000.00 and, our third year, we were up to $3,000,000.00.

That third year, there were only three phone calls to the police, and 85% of the people in the community were working and paying taxes instead of being on assistance. We won major awards— including the Presidential Points of Light Award—and we were invited by Congress to share the story of how we achieved our success.

It all was about God working with our hearts filled with His love. And we are still going. We have tried many things. Some did not work and we let them go. The things that worked, we kept.

We used the "Whole Man" concept, (which is in the Bible). That means "physical, intellectual, and spiritual." Men and women need to be in good physical condition, get an education, and know God. That foundation will stand up under any conditions… and circumstances.

I divided my time between our projects in San Diego and Los Angeles, spending about 10 days a month in San Diego, and the remainder on L.A. working with gangs. The goal was to prevent further polarization among the gangs.

One of the young guys I connected with was a guy named Brian Weaver. He was a part of a notorious gang known as The Bloods. He had lived alone in the "projects" in Watts since he was just 12 years old. He was living by the neighborhood's values—not society's values. He had learned some values—how to be loyal and efficient—but his road to prison was paved by "conspiracy to procure and distribute illegal drugs." He only spent three years behind bars, because he was too young to be imprisoned over the long term.

If you think that gang members are just a bunch of underachievers who have no chance at a successful life, Brian Weaver would prove you wrong. Brian was an achiever who simply had no opportunity to prove that he could achieve. He was trapped. But, working together, we set him free from that trap!

I offered Brian a job...only $200 a month...but he took it. It was less than he had been making through his "other" activities—illicit ones—but he was smart enough to know that a simple honest job just might turn his life around. It did! Brian has helped me in ways I can't begin to measure!

The vital lesson I've learned through my work with kids is, "You have to mean what you say." Your word has to be good. And it's vital to back up words with actions. This is important no matter if you are working with gangs, or a Scout Troop, or a third-grade Sunday School class. The gang members I chose to serve didn't expect me to stay. But when I told them, "I'll be here; get used to my face," I meant it.

Throughout my life, I have been inspired by so many others who backed up their words with actions. Martin Luther King, Jr., Robert F. Kennedy, the brave men and women who serve in our armed forces—and so many others—risk their lives to make a difference in the world. Tragically, we have lost too many of them.

But as long as I'm here, I'm going to care…and I'm going to put my caring into action.

Rosey's Rose-Colored Gem

Get involved! You will be as big a winner as the people you help!

Chapter Sixteen

In Trouble With The Law

"Resist this war on God, freedom of religion and freedom of speech."

—Benjamin Carson, MD

I've made some major mistakes in my life—one of them was just a couple of years ago. At least, it was a mistake in the eyes of my local Starbucks manager…even if it wasn't a mistake in my own eyes. But that mistake almost got me in trouble with the police.

My first mistake was that I thought when I walked through the door at Starbucks to get my coffee—and other customers recognized me and said "Hi," even after all these years—I could actually talk to those customers. I thought I had Freedom of Speech, as guaranteed by the First Amendment of the U.S. Constitution.

Often, at their invitation, I would begin to talk to them about life, about football, about my current work, and about their lives. No real problem so far. The cops had not yet been called.

Then I made my second mistake. I began to chat with them about what was really important to me—my faith. I told them about the secret to eternal life. Life that would never end.

Often when I went there alone, I would treat the person standing in line behind me. They always accepted my offer with gratitude. Then I would say, "May I ask you a serious question? If you died today, do you think you would go to heaven?"

Most of them would answer with something like, "I think so, because I'm a good person."

I respond with, "I know that sounds like it should be enough, but it's not. That's because we're not as perfect as we'd like to be. But if I told you that you already have a free ticket to heaven, would you take it?"

If they say, "Yes," I continue, and I explain to them where Jesus fits into all of this—and I lead them in a simple prayer. If their answer is "No," I politely end the conversation.

Well, somewhere along the line, one of the customers didn't like it that I approached that subject.

I went there a few days later with my daughter, Sherryl, who was visiting from out-of-town. I introduced her to the Baristas as we stood in line. After we were served and seated, the manager approached us and asked to speak to Sherryl. He led her to an area away from most of the crowd. She told me about their conversation later.

"That's your father, right?"

"Yes, he is," she responded.

"Well, he's harassing the other customers."

"Really? How is he doing that?"

"He's hassling them about religion. He's trying to convert them, or something."

She asked, "Is that a problem?"

He said, "Yes, in our establishment, it is. He has to stop."

When we got home, Sherryl gave me all the details of the conversation.

The next evening, I went walking by myself, with the intention of stopping by Starbucks to ask some questions. I asked to speak to the manager. He wasn't there, so the assistant manager came over to talk with me.

"We don't want you in our store," she said bluntly.

"Why not?

She ignored my question and said, "I'm sorry, but we just can't serve you." She pointed to a rather unfriendly sign that read, "We reserve the right to refuse service to anyone."

A couple at a nearby table overheard the conservation, so I asked them for their names. The woman gave me hers. I wanted to connect with someone who witnessed the events that were unfolding.

The assistant manager interrupted. "We've asked you to leave." She followed that with a threat to call the police.

Now, I don't know about you, but I have countless friends who have died in far-flung places around the world to defend our freedoms, including certain rights guaranteed by the First Amendment to our Constitution. Speech is one of them.

And, at that moment, I felt that someone was trying to take my freedoms away from me. At a Starbucks in Brentwood, of all places.

Not wanting to cause a scene, I walked out the door, accompanied by the assistant manager and a guard, and I stood by a parking meter.

"Is this where your property ends?" I asked her. "Because if you don't own the sidewalk or the parking meters or the street, I have the right to be here."

Readers, I know that this doesn't sound much like typical "Rosey," but at that moment, I wasn't seeing the world through my "Rosey-colored Glasses."

There are times when businesses don't understand that there are certain ways that businesses have to do business. This seemed to me to be one of those times—I was "uninvited" to be a customer of that particular Starbucks because I was engaging in conversations with other customers about what I see as "Eternal" matters.

A few minutes later, a squad car drove up. Two officers got out of the car and approached me.

They greeted me and I held out my wrists so they could handcuff me. "I'm ready," I offered.

They laughed. "Mr. Grier, we're not going to arrest you."

I was puzzled, "You mean I'm not going to jail? I thought that's why you're here."

"No, we're just here to find out what's going on."

"So I'm not under arrest?" I asked again to clarify the issue.

"No, this is a civil matter. You haven't committed a crime."

"How can they throw me out because I want to talk about God?"

"Well," one officer replied, "as I'm sure you know, they have the right to refuse service to anyone."

I thought about all the other times in my life that I had been "refused service." Not pleasant thoughts. That was the "old America." I thought I was living in the new America. Tolerance was supposed to be our accepted way of life.

A neighbor passed by and asked, "What are you doing here, Rosey? And what are the police doing here?"

I told her, "I got kicked out. They don't approve of me talking about God. I'm not welcome at Starbucks."

The policemen listened to all of this very politely. Then out of nowhere, I asked the officers, "Do you mind if I pray for you?

They both replied, "Fine. No problem."

So I did. I prayed for wisdom. I prayed for their safety on the job. I prayed for their families.

They thanked me, then they said, "Have a good day, Mr. Grier."

We parted company, but as I stood there in front of Starbucks, I wondered, "What has happened in our country? Why have we replaced the Ten Commandments in schools with metal detectors? Why have we become so adversarial?"

I went home, and thought about the past few days. I thought some more. And I thought some more.

A major thought that suddenly occurred to me was: *All my life I've played defense. All my life I've defended people who are overlooked—especially gang members and the elderly. Maybe it's time I go on the offensive. Maybe I should play offense instead of defense.*

The more I thought about it, the more I agreed with myself! I was convinced that—while there are several things I can comfortably *defend*—there are exactly two areas where *offense* is required.

The first one is human rights, especially my rights as guaranteed by the Bill of Rights and protected by law.

The second is my faith. And by that, I don't simply mean my First Amendment right to "Freedom of Religion." I mean, I take the biblical commandment to "Go into all the world and preach the Gospel to everyone" literally. Jesus said that, and he meant those words for me. To me, "all the world" includes a certain Starbucks in Brentwood. It means anywhere that I am at any moment in time.

Finally, after much deliberation, I went on the offensive and called an attorney. He sent a letter to the company headquarters in Seattle. In it, he stated that I intended to sue them for 33 million dollars. (I personally picked that number because that's how old Jesus was when he was crucified.)

That got their attention immediately, and a couple of executives flew down to LA from Seattle. They met my lawyer and me at the office.

"What authority do you have," I asked them, "to suppress my freedom of speech? What right do you have to humiliate and insult me publicly…in front of my neighbors?"

"Mr. Grier, our company gives generously to the Urban League," was their response.

I could not believe what I was hearing! It's strange—seems like people try to justify what they are doing by pointing out the wonderful things they are doing for the Black community.

"I didn't ask you what you do for 'my people.' I asked why you think you have the right to restrict my speech and humiliate me publicly. I've seen other people come into Starbucks yelling and cussing and abusing your Baristas. I came in quietly. I struck up conversations with other customers. And you're going to throw me out because I bring in Good News?"

They had no response.

We eventually established a truce, and, of course, I never followed through on my threat to sue them in court for $33 million. In some respects I regret that decision. On the other hand, going on the offensive doesn't always have to lead to war. I learned that it can lead to peace!

Rosey's Rose-Colored Gem

Instead of playing the game of life on the defense, consider playing offense. There are things in your world that are worth defending, of course, but there are other things that are worth advancing. That requires offense. And sometimes, offense can be offensive to people. It can offend them. But if your cause is truly significant and worthwhile, that is a chance worth taking.

Chapter Seventeen

Pain Is A Part Of Life

"The pain of parting is nothing to the joy of meeting again."

—Charles Dickens

Because I believe that the teachings of the Bible are the Word of God, and because I have placed my faith and trust in Jesus Christ, I am confident that life is divided into two unequal parts. There is "Life before Death," and "Life after Death."

Life before death is, thankfully, very short, all things considered. It is full of disappointments, suffering, uncertainty, and pain.

Life after death is life without end. We are no longer confronted by disappointments. Uncertainty is replaced with certainty. Suffering and pain are banished forever.

It is that hope of Eternal Life through Jesus that has kept me going when life throws challenges and heartbreaks at me.

I have witnessed a lot of death.

I saw a man gunned down on the streets of Cuthbert, Georgia, while I was still an innocent child. Much of my innocence was stolen from me on that day.

I experienced the deaths of my brothers and sisters throughout my life.

My wonderful parents have been gone for many years.

My dear friend, Bobby, was tragically cut down before he had the opportunity to do wonderful things for his countrymen. Whatever "innocence" I still had left on that day was taken away forever.

Jackie, my special buddy, my "partner in crime," left our world long before I ever thought she would. I actually believed that she was invincible… even though I knew better.

Then there were the three amazing guys who formed three-fourths of the Fearsome Foursome of the Los Angeles Rams. We remained friends long after our playing days were over. The other guys played for a varying number of years after my injury took me out of the game and led me to my next journey with Bobby Kennedy.

But Lamar J. Lundy, Jr., Merlin Olsen, and Deacon Jones are all gone. I miss my friends.

I have a wonderful daughter named Sherryl, from a former relationship when I was in college. Since I was away in college and played college and pro football, I traveled a lot and we did not have the opportunity to grow and get to know each other. My first wife had a daughter named Denise, and the two mothers made it difficult for Sherryl and me to have a good relationship.

I am so thankful that many years ago, we were able to spend more time together. And though we are thousands of miles apart, we talk weekly and see each other as frequently as we can. Sherryl is a strong believer and is a great support to things I am doing in my life. She gave me two grandchildren, Kimberly and Keith, and they have given me three great-grandchildren: Michael, Keith, Jr. and Kayla. What great gifts from God!

Along the way, Margie became very ill. I decided I needed to recruit a team of caring individuals to pray for her. I thought about a lady I had met approximately twenty-three years earlier named Cydnee. I did not have a recent phone number for her, but I knew that she had worked for the Wichita Public School System. I got her classroom number from their directory, and asked her to join in praying for Margie and me. When Margie had passed, I called a few weeks later and gave her the news.

It was on June 10, 2011, that I lost Margie to cancer. Before she died, the nurse came and told me that Margie was asking her, "Am I going to die?"

So I said, "I'll go talk to her."

I went into Margie's room and I said to her, "We are doing everything we can to keep the pain down. Is there *anything* you would like to talk to me about?"

Her response was, "No, but I am concerned about the children."

I responded, "You have taught Rosey and me how to take care of ourselves and if you want to keep fighting, we will fight with you. If you want to go home and be with the Lord, we will be okay. What do you want to do?"

She said, "I want to go home and be with the Lord." I was shaking when she said that.

I went in the other room and cried.

Later, I walked by her room and she was lying in bed, drinking a milkshake. I felt good that she wasn't going anywhere. About an hour later, the nurse came to me and said, "She's gone." I went in the room and looked at her, and I could see that she was no longer breathing. I touched her.

Then I tried to call my son, Rosey, but couldn't reach him. I called his ex-wife, Tescia, and she said, "I'm on my way." I also called my nephew, Robert Blackwell, and he came, too. They got there quickly.

Then Rosey, Jr. called me. He said, "Dad, I'm on my way." It seemed to be taking him a long time. So I decided to call him again. He answered the phone and I asked him if he was okay. He said, "Dad, it's like mom is in the car with me. I can feel her spirit." I was relieved that he seemed to be handling the loss of his mom. He arrived and said, "Dad, sit down. I will take care of everything." And he did.

The good news is, as certain as pain is a part of life, so are recovery and healing. The love of my daughter, Sherryl, and her children, Keith and Kimberly, and my son, Rosey, Jr., and his children Amai Cyan and Roosevelt Kennedy III, have helped me heal.

My basic plan was to just sit in my corner at home and read the Bible. One day, I looked in the closet and I spotted my guitar. I had not played it for about six years. I started playing the guitar again and writing songs.

I went to a Thanksgiving dinner that our family had been going to for 26 years, and I began to go out more—not just sitting around the house.

People were continually talking to me about traveling, but I was not interested in that at all. I had done considerable traveling most of my life.

Eighteen months passed, and I decided that I would try to look up Cydnee—the woman from Wichita who had prayed for Margie—and see if she had changed. I thought about going a couple of times but would change my mind. My assistant helped me get a non-refundable ticket to Wichita, so I didn't change my mind this time.

When I arrived at the airport in Wichita, I spotted her before she saw me. I called out her name and she came over to me...and a revelation occurred. She had matured, but looked even better than before. She was beautiful, and her weight was beautiful. My life changed in that moment!

The Bible says, "It is not good for man to live alone." I personally learned that the Bible is 100% correct regarding that observation. I am definitely the kind of guy who values—actually needs—a faithful, loving woman in my life.

Cydnee, her family, and I had initially met at a conference in Oklahoma back in 1991. Cyd was a kindergarten teacher living in Wichita, Kansas.

Throughout the years, I would occasionally fly to Wichita for events with the World Impact urban ministry. Every time I came to Wichita, I would notice that Cydnee and her family were always at events and were always involved in the community. She has the same love for children that I do, and she has always helped to make things better.

We decided to start "courting" long distance. I would have her fly to California when she would have breaks at school. We talked on the phone two or three times daily and would do devotions on the phone at night with each other.

Before long it just seemed like everything began to click. I felt like Cydnee was the one woman who could help bring joy and healing back into my life. We got married on April 30, 2013. She finished the school year in Wichita, and retired from teaching. Then she came to Los Angeles shortly after I finished remodeling the condo.

Cyd is a very delightful, Godly lady who shares my ministry interests. Our life plan is to serve God and people together for as many years as God gives us. We are praying to God that all of our children will be part of the family of God. Cydnee's family has embraced our marriage with love and respect.

Yes, pain is a very real part of life on this earth. But the LOVE of God and other people can—and will—see you through.

Rosey's Rose-Colored Gem

Count your blessings while you can. Remember that people—not things—are your greatest blessings. Value and appreciate the people in your life while they are still with you, and tell them so!

Chapter Eighteen

A Joyful Surprise!

"You don't choose your family.

They are God's gift to you, as you are to them."

—Desmond Tutu

Even life's biggest surprises can be Rosey-colored—if you are willing to look at them through my glasses. There can be joy in the unexpected.

After Margie died in 2011, and before I married Cydnee, I became a lonely man…more lonely than I ever imagined possible. To fill the void, I tried to add new interests and new activities to my schedule. Since I've always loved music and theatre, I decided to include music and writing songs in my life plan. That seemed logical, and it led to the recording studio, where I created a new CD titled, *Let the Old Man Play.*

I am blessed with a daughter and a son who both understand and accept my whims. So when I asked my son, Rosey, to accompany me to the taping of a game show in LA, he agreed without hesitation. I'm sure he was thinking, "My old man needs me. That's cool."

During intermission, I was standing in line to get a soda when a woman walked up to me and struck up a conversation.

"You're Rosey Grier, right?"

"Yes, that's right."

"I want you to know I was so in love with Margie's son."

"Really?" I was immediately fascinated. I spotted Rosey, Jr., and called him over. "Rosey, this lady says that she was totally in love with you." Rosey, Jr. looked at her and walked away

The woman broke in right away. "No, not this son. Margie's other son, Michael Steven Pollard."

I stood there with an expression on my face that obviously said, "Huh?"

"Your wife is Margie, right?" she asked.

"That's right," I replied. "But she passed away about a year ago."

"Well, I am very sorry to hear that, Mr. Grier. But it was her other son, Michael, whom I loved."

After further probing, I asked my niece, Nikki, to get information from the lady on how I could contact the family.

She brought me the phone number of Denise Walton, Margie's daughter and Michael's sister. I have never once heard her name mentioned.

I couldn't wait until 8:30 the next morning, Saturday, to call Denise. And when I did call her, I discovered some very interesting facts that left me in a state of complete shock.

Denise said she had been waiting for a call for over forty years. I asked her if she could substantiate that she was really Margie's daughter. She said that she would meet us anywhere with that information. I told her, "We will come to your house."

Rosey, Jr. and I went to Denise and Ron's home, and she had documents and pictures of the three young children with Margie, (before she left them), to prove she was Margie's daughter. We all looked at one another and did not know what to say. Rosey, Jr. looked at the pictures and said, "It's mom, all right."

That day, we learned for certain that Margie, my wife of more than 40 years, had been married previously, and she had given birth to—not just one son, but—three children. One was a girl—Denise—and two were boys, Michael and Bobbie. One of the sons, Michael, died shortly after Margie did.

What Rosey, Jr. and I could not believe is that my wife—his mom—had kept this secret for all those years. We had no idea!

We have never met the father of Margie's other children, but since this amazing revelation became known, we have met her two surviving children, Denise and Bobbie. In fact, even though they are Margie's children with another man, we have accepted them as part of the family and have become very close, especially with Denise. Rosey, Jr. is pleased to have discovered a half-brother and half-sister, and he enjoys spending time with them.

Denise told us that when she turned 35, she sent a registered letter to Margie, hoping to see her birth mom again. Denise had some medical questions, and she needed Margie to help with the answers. Margie never responded.

Of course, a big question keeps crossing my mind. Why did Margie lie and say she had no other children? Why so many other deceptions?

It was heartbreaking to me that Margie completely abandoned her children when Denise was only three years old. She had chosen to go to court and give up her children. She never saw them again, nor had she ever tried to contact them.

The courts told her she could not see her children and was giving up her parental rights. She was prepared to live with that. The fact that they were so young at the time she deserted them is what shocked me. Inconceivable! They would see Margie on TV with me, talking about how important family was, and know that she was their mom.

When Denise found out as a child that Margie had Rosey, Jr., she thought that Margie abandoned her because she was a girl and that Margie didn't like her for that reason.

All I know for sure is that I love them now—but I wish I had known about them all those years. We were all cheated.

Rosey's Rose-Colored Gem

A surprise in life—one that may seem to be a valley at first—may turn out to be a summit from which all of the world looks better and brighter! Margie's secret became our blessing. I hope something as wonderful happens to you—even if it's completely unexpected. I hope it brings you joy!

Chapter Nineteen

Meaning Something

"The sole meaning of life is to serve the Creator of humanity.

It's not about us, it's about Him."

—Rosey Grier

When I look at life through my Rosey-colored glasses, I see that life is not about "Me, Me, Me." It's really about "We, We, We." It's about all of us working together to solve problems. It's about setting aside our differences to find common ground to make a difference.

Think about this: Can you think of anyone you know who you'd want to die of cancer? If your answer is "no," would that tell you that "we, we, we" means that we support research to find cures for prostate cancer, breast cancer, leukemia, and every other cancer.

Do you want children to starve? Do you want kids not to get educated? Of course not!

I believe that the best and highest legacy to which anyone can aspire is to be remembered as someone who cared. Someone who was unselfishly dedicated to making life better for others who may not have been able to go it alone. As the famous song lyrics by Jimmy Durante suggested—"Make someone happy…Make just one someone happy…And you will be happy, too."

There are two groups to which I have specifically and purposefully dedicated my life in recent years. One is kids, who need all the love, support, and encouragement they can possibly get. The other is the elderly—senior citizens—who often live their last years in loneliness and despair. Honestly, I don't just "care" about these two groups; my heart often breaks for them.

I told you about my work with street gangs and the meaning I've personally discovered through that endeavor. I really want their lives to be fulfilled.

But there are kids who need our attention who are not drawn into crime and violence and gang warfare. They are simply everyday kids who need to gain a sense of achievement.

Kids who are successful in some area of life often have a better chance of escaping the downward spiral that could engulf them in a future filled with drugs or alcohol. Sports, music, and art offer opportunities for kids to excel. But what about kids who can't carry a ball, carry a tune, or even draw stick figures? They need opportunities, too.

I have partnered with my friend of more than 65 years, Wallace "Wally" Choice, to create something he calls the "Industry of Athletics." Wally and I have talked on the phone frequently for decades, so it made obvious sense to partner with him on something significant.

Wally and I met on the track field in high school and served in the Army together. He went to Indiana University and was the first African-American to be selected at the captain of a Big Ten basketball team. After college, Wally played with the Harlem Globetrotters. Then he taught English for many years at Montclair High School in New Jersey.

The Industry of Athletics was Wally's idea more than thirty years ago. He realized that not every high school student can be a sports star, but they can all excel in something. He concluded that it would be worthwhile to introduce kids to other job opportunities related to sports. After all, there are managers, trainers, and physical therapists related to every sport. There are reporters, sportscasters, photographers, videographers, and statisticians in service on every field or court of any and every sport.

Wally reasoned, "Athletes are already established on their path. But there are so many other ways to become meaningfully involved in the broader 'industry' of athletics."

Many kids, especially in the urban areas that have professional teams, can't afford to buy tickets to games. The Industry of Athletics allows kids to attend games, and it gives them meaningful things to do. They can "shadow" sportscasters, trainers, and equipment people, and hang around them to learn. They can begin to build marketable skills.

And it works! Interestingly, one of Wally's students at Montclair, Aubrey Lewis, was one of New Jersey's greatest high school athletes. Aubrey became the first Black to be named captain of an athletic team at Notre Dame and was a noted track and football star. Lewis was inducted into the New Jersey Hall of Fame in 2003.

Wally and I have been able to gain support for IOA. We are still building this organization, and there is much more to be accomplished.

The other group I care deeply about is our nation's senior citizens. Of course, I realize that you might be laughing right now. That's because I'm 82 years old, so it has probably dawned on you that I am a senior citizen, too.

But I am not a typical person of my age. I am still healthy, I am still physically active, I am still employed in a meaningful job, and I am not alone—I am married and have children and grandchildren who are an important part of my daily life.

There are many others, however, who are not as blessed. They live lonely lives in lonely places, without much attention or companionship.

It was actually some former street gang members who brought the needs of seniors to my attention many years ago. The kids suggested that we have a special event—a party—for them. We sent our invitees large cans of popcorn as invitations to a "Senior Cotillion." That's a prom-like event that was popular years ago—a ball at which young ladies were introduced to society.

Our ladies (and gentlemen) weren't young anymore, but you'd better believe they loved being honored and "introduced!" We were able to pull off this wonderful evening because the Milken Family Foundation gave us $15,000 to cover our costs.

I believe that all human beings, no matter what age, education, or personal history needs a support group behind them. And, if not a group, at least a cheerleader…someone who says, "I'm here for you. I'm behind you. I care."

I choose to be that supporter—that cheerleader.

Rosey's Rose-Colored Gem

Never give up on anyone. Everyone has something to contribute to the greater good of humanity. You may be the perfect person to help bring out special qualities in someone else!

Chapter Twenty

I'll Take You There

"Ain't nobody cryin'. Ain't nobody worried.
No smilin' faces lyin' to the races...I'll take you there!
Just take me by the hand. Let me lead the way...
I'll take you there!"

—The Staple Singers (MetroLyrics)

On occasion, a few of my friends have ridiculed me for openly wearing my Rosey-colored glasses. They say, "Rosey, you've had as many bad things happen to you as anyone we know. How can you possibly remain so positive?"

I tell them, "It's really very simple. There are three ways to look at life."

They stare at me with puzzled expressions on their faces.

"First," I explain, "there are those things that just 'happen' to you. There is really nothing you can do about it except trust God in all circumstances."

Occasionally, I get an "Amen."

"Second, there are those things that you *make* happen in your life. But even that doesn't always work out the way you hoped. Again, in my own life, I have learned to trust God through any and every joy or disappointment."

My friends nod their heads in understanding and agreement.

"Finally, there are those wonderful things I *know* are *going* to happen! And I fully trust God once again. Because He's the one who is going to allow them to happen."

I really think I've been blessed with an interesting life. I've had some very special opportunities that I never thought would come my way.

I am thankful that I was born into a loving family—to parents who cared about making sure I was able to get an education.

I am thankful that I was able to play the greatest game ever invented, and play it at the high school, college, and pro levels... with some amazing teammates!

I am thankful for the interesting and varied career that followed my NFL playing days—politics, music, television, movies, and my work with Michael Milken.

I am thankful for my family—for Margie, my children, and my grandchildren—and for the new family I met through the joy of my marriage to Cydnee.

I am thankful that I had the opportunity to serve a great man in Bobby Kennedy. The tragedy that "happened" right before my eyes will never diminish the many things he accomplished.

I am thankful for my dear friend, Jackie. I loved her like a sister. We had fun. We respected each other. We mutually cared about the larger world. We had shared pain and loss…some of it together. And we were open enough with each other to share our hearts.

And as to O.J., I am thankful I had to opportunity to give him spiritual guidance. I cared about him as a man. I still do today. He never confessed anything to me—not even the simplest sin. I think he realizes, as the Bible says, that ALL have sinned…all of us have messed up…and we all have "missed the mark"—the target that is the standard God has set for us. I believe with all my heart that he also understands that confession and faith in Jesus Christ are the only things that can bridge the gap between death and life that goes on forever.

The Bible explains it very clearly in a verse that has been called out on huge signs behind the goal posts in thousands of football games. It's John 3:16. "For God so loved the world that he gave his one and only Son, that whoever believes in him shall not perish but have eternal life."

That's from a translation of the ancient Greek texts known as the New International Version (NIV). It doesn't matter which translation you read. It all comes down to the same thing. God loved the world. He sent his Son.

I personalize it and say: "For God loved Rosey Grier, a football player from Georgia, so much that he gave his one and only Son, Jesus, that if Rosey simply believes in him, Rosey will never die, but will have eternal life."

And that, dear friends, is the real reason why I see life though Rosey-colored glasses. I believe that, because of the sacrifice and resurrection of Jesus Christ, something very wonderful is going to happen to me in the future.

Through these pages, I haven't been trying to convince you that you must get a college education. I'm not saying you should or shouldn't pursue sports, or business, or politics. I'm not saying how you should vote. You need to follow the dreams and goals that are right for you. The path that suits your talents, abilities, and interests is the only one worth pursuing.

But what I am saying is, no matter what your achievements may be, no matter how many victories are in your win column, no matter how much money you've accumulated, and yes, even how many people you've helped, when you get to the end of your life, none of that will really count for anything.

I believe what really matters when we leave this earth is, "Did we accept God's free and priceless gift to us? Did we come to the point where we realized and believed that, through the life, death, and resurrection of his Son, Jesus Christ, we could spend eternity in the presence of Almighty God?

I hope that this book will help you realize just how important you are. If things should go wrong, there's a place you can go to find help and a friend when you need it.

You have angels all around you and their purpose is to help you stay on the "narrow road" that leads to eternal life.

My prayer is that this story has somehow helped you discover the significant questions of life – and the answers to them.

Rosey's Rose-Colored Gem

As wonderful as Life can be—even with all its challenges and sorrows, Everlasting Life with God is even more wonderful!

BONUS CHAPTER

Q & A
With Rosey

Nearly every day of my life, I get involved in conversations with people who have questions for me. I'd like to share some of these questions, along with the answers I have offered.

Q) What are your favorite football memories from high school, Penn State, and the NFL?

A) I have lots of memories…and most are wonderful!

My best memories of high school football include beating Roselle Park during the Thanksgiving game. John Cramer, who just had one arm (due to a birth defect), caught the winning touchdown!

In college, I advanced from sitting on the bench to playing on both sides of the line of scrimmage—offense and defense.

In the NFL, winning the "outstanding player" of the game, which was played in the mud at the Polo grounds in 1955. Along with that, playing in the first "overtime" game in football; also, playing in the World Championship Game. It went into overtime and was called "The Greatest Game Ever Played" (But we lost that game to the Baltimore Colts.)

There are other memories, of course, that aren't so pleasant.

In high school, I got my back hurt in practice and was sent to the Doctor to get a shot to numb the pain—so I could play in the game the next day. It took me a while to get my walk back.

In college—I was denied permission to play in the East-West game because of my color. That situation sure has changed!

In the NFL, by biggest disappointment was getting from the NY Giants to the LA Rams—and the Rams players did not get along.

Q) Did you ever feel that the Kennedy's flaunted their position, power, prestige or money to get what they wanted?

A) No, honestly, not at all. I'm not sure why this is, but for the most part, the Kennedy's wanted what was right for others…what was right for America.

Q) Are you related to the beautiful actress Pam Grier

A) Pam and I never did the research as to whether we were cousins or not, but we said we were.

Q) Do you expect us to believe that you could spend so much time visiting O.J. Simpson in prison—up to three times a week—

and he would never admit his guilt to you?

A)   As I told the lawyers, as I told the guards, as I told the press, and as I'm telling you now, my only job was to share the Word of God with a man in great personal pain. God knew his heart, and the jury decided he was innocent. As to the civil trial, I have questions....

Q)   Do you, today, consider yourself to be a member of the Republican Party?

A)   I consider myself, above all, to be a man who fully accepts what the Bible teaches. It is the ultimate guide for my life. Which political party I affiliate with—or which political party you affiliate with—really doesn't matter. What matters is, which party...which philosophy...which platform, most closely aligns with the teaching of Jesus? Is any party perfect? No. That will never happen, because people invented politics. Does man have all the answers? No. Given those realities, for me, it's Bible First, Constitution Second, and Everything Else (such as Political Parties) Third. So I will vote for those candidates for office who most convincingly align their positions with my spiritual and moral priorities. If another "Ronald Reagan" type of person came along, I'd vote for him or her. If another "Robert F. Kennedy" type of person surfaced, I'd vote for him or her. Just don't sell out on me, ya hear?

APPENDIX

The "Cast Of Characters"

Historical background on some of the people mentioned in this book:

Bill Berry—In charge of movement and security for the RFK campaign. He placed me in charge of Ethel (she was 6 months pregnant).

Joan Braden—Hostess and friend to high-ranking Washington figures; she arranged for my 1st active support to a political campaign with RFK.

Sam Cook—Great gospel singer who migrated to pop music, later killed.

Senator John Glenn—First U.S. astronaut to orbit the earth (and flew on the Space Shuttle at age 77, becoming the oldest person in space). He was elected U.S. Senator from Ohio and was the first candidate outside the Kennedy family that Jackie Kennedy endorsed.

Averell Harriman—US Ambassador-at-large, 1965-68.

Billy Graham—Renowned American evangelist.

Rafer Johnson—Second Black Olympic Decathlon winner; carried the Olympic Torch in the LA Opening Ceremonies in 1984.

Deacon Jones—Greatest defensive end in football, nicknamed the "Secretary of Defense." Came up with "sacking" the quarterback; part of the Fearsome Foursome; member of the Hall of Fame.

Lamar Lundy—Defensive end for LA Rams, part of the Fearsome Foursome.

Frank Mankiewicz—spokesman and press aide for RFK.

Howard Metzenbaum—Politician John Glenn defeated in Ohio for Senate seat in Washington, DC; later he became a Senator from Ohio.

Merlin Olsen—One of the all-time great defensive tackles; named to the Hall of Fame; a wonderful philanthropist.

George Plimpton—A journalist and decathlete; tried to get the gun away from Sirhan Sirhan, but could not, so I took it out of his hand and put it in my pocket.

Pierre Salinger—Spokesman for JFK.

Paul Schrade—Representative for the United Auto Workers; shot at the assassination of RFK.

Robert Shapiro—Lawyer for O.J. Simpson who brought the legal team together.

Sirhan Sirhan—Assassinated RFK; was given a life sentence.

O.C. Smith—American musician, wrote "Little Green Apples."

Ethel Waters—Great gospel singer, she played my mom on a "Daniel Boone" episode.

Justice Byron "Whizzer" White—Great football player, Justice of the Supreme Court of the United States.

Acknowledgments

There are so many people who actively participate in the development of a book. I hope I have remembered them all!

First, I would like to thank my wife, Lady Cydnee, and my assistant, Lady Jessica Raminfard, for their great resolve in helping me communicate my story. Jessica, I know your head must be spinning because you've gone in a thousand directions, but you've been a game player every step of the way.

I would also like to thank my son, Rosey Grier, Jr., and my attorney, Bob Johnson, for setting up the writing contract so that we have a clear understanding of how we were to spend resources to get the book done.

I'd like to thank Steve Gottry for his fine efforts and stirring the soup to create a book that gives a vital message to so many who are searching for answers. He has done a great job in laying out the stories to keep the interest of my readers, and has told the stories with dignity. I pray that he and his family experience greatness in their lives.

I also want express my gratitude to the graphic designers and book cover designers and photographers for their efforts and time in bringing the book to life.

The book was written to be faith-based. Our prayers are that everyone who reads this book will be blessed and encouraged to step out and make a difference in our society. One man or one woman can change the course of our nation. Why not you? You have been gifted with the skills and talent to make a great contribution. There is no one better than you, and each one of you has a uniqueness that is rare and is surely needed in our society today. Can I hear an "Amen?"

I am inspired by the pictures of all the men and women I see on my office walls who have made great contributions to our society. Many of them you don't know and have never heard of, but they all made a difference by being themselves.

You don't have to be a President, or Oprah Winfrey, or Brian Weaver to make a difference in our society. What you have to possess is the boldness to speak what you are thinking. It takes courage to speak your mind, but that shouldn't stop you if you feel that is right!

About The Author

Roosevelt Grier was born in 1932 in Cuthbert, Georgia, into a family of eleven brothers and sisters.

He attended Penn State University, where he was the track team captain as well as a college football All-American. It was at Penn State that Rosey began his prominent membership of Alpha Phi Alpha, the first intercollegiate Greek-letter fraternity established for African-Americans. Rosey moved on to play professional football for the New York Giants (1955-1962) and the Los Angeles Rams (1962-1967).

Rosey has received countless honors and awards, including All-American both in high school and at Penn State University. He was named All-Pro with the New York Giants one time, played in five World Championship games, and was a prominent member of the most honored defensive line in the history of professional football—"The Fearsome Foursome."

In addition to sports, Rosey has excelled in numerous fields, including public relations and the recording industry. Television viewers have seen him on numerous hit shows such as *The Smothers Brothers* and *Quincy*.

Feature film credits include *Roots, Skyjacked, In Cold Blood,* and *Carter's Army.*

Rosey is also a best-selling author whose books include *Shooting Star, All-American Heroes, Winning, Rosey: The Gentle Giant (his auto-biography), and Needlepoint For Men.*

In November of 1974, his needlepoint work was featured on the cover of the renowned *Saturday Evening Post*.

He recently released his third album entitled *Rosey Grier— Let The Ol' Man Play. Life Through Rosey-Colored Glasses* is his sixth book.

As a humanitarian, Rosey is the co-founder (along with Estean Lenyoun) of American Neighborhood Enterprises (ANE). He is Acting Chairman of the Board for an offshoot of ANE, "Impact Urban America," as well. These enterprises are an alliance of real estate development and construction companies committed to providing job training, employment, first-time buyer programs, and affordable housing for disadvantaged, underprivileged and at-risk persons in the inner-cities of our nation.

Rosey is Founder and Chairman of "Giant Step," a non-profit program designed to give disadvantaged youth job training as well as to provide housing for senior citizens. Along with Giant Step, he has created and developed a program that enhances spiritual awareness and self-esteem in underprivileged inner city youth known as, "Rosey Grier's Are You Committed?"

Rosey is a valued friend of the powerful as well as the less fortunate. As a concerned citizen and spokesman for the elderly and inner-city youth of America, Rosey has been the recipient of numerous national honors and White House invitations from several Presidents of the United States. A political activist, Rosey was at the Ambassador Hotel the night Sirhan Sirhan assassinated Senator Robert F. Kennedy. He helped apprehend Sirhan and took the gun out of his hand. Rosey wept with our nation over the loss of a great leader.

He has also received resolutions of commendation from the California State Assembly, The Los Angeles City Council, the late Los Angles Mayor-Elect Tom Bradley, and the Board of Supervisors of Orange County.

Other honors have included Master of Ceremonies for the Special Olympics (1970-1983), the Watson Award from IBM and the B'nai B'rith Champion of Youth. His additional accolades consist of the National Football League Humanitarian Award and the Penn State Alumnus of the Year.

In 1981, Rosey was awarded an honorary Doctorate of the Letter of Law from Oral Roberts University, where he once sat on the Board of Regents. He has also served on the boards of numerous other organizations and institutions, including World Impact, The Fundamental Foundation, The Tuberculosis and Respiratory Disease Association of Los Angeles County, and the State Athletic Commission for California.

Currently, Rosey works on a number of projects at the Milken Family Foundation, a non-profit organization founded by Michael and Lowell Milken. The foundation is dedicated to promoting education, advancing medical care, and doing research. He invests a large amount of time and effort on behalf of The Prostate Cancer Foundation, an organization founded by Mike Milken, that is dedicated to the research for prevention and cure of prostate cancer.

Mr. Grier has a daughter and a son—Sherryl Tubbs and Roosevelt Kennedy Grier. He also has four grandchildren: Amai, Roosevelt "Roro," Keith Tubbs, and Kimberly Tubbs.

Rosey has been married since April of 2013. He was blessed to marry Cydnee (Stillwaugh) Grier, a Kansas schoolteacher.

Footnotes

[1] Adapted from Wikipedia.

(We will also need to credit song lyrics.)

CPSIA information can be obtained
at www.ICGtesting.com
Printed in the USA
LVHW031752211119
638114LV00014B/911/P